PHENOMENA

SACRED MOMENTS, MESSAGES, MEMORIES
& OTHER SH*T I CAN'T EXPLAIN

JOHN ST. AUGUSTINE

PHENOMENA
SACRED MOMENTS, MESSAGES, MEMORIES
& OTHER SH*T I CAN'T EXPLAIN

JOHN ST. AUGUSTINE

AURORA PUBLISHING
2020

First Printing: 2020
ISBN 978-0-359-23136-2

Photo/Image Credits: Pg. 17 NEIU Pg. 80 Public Domain Pg. 40 & 52
Sue Lyon Pg. 60, 113, 122, 184, 194 & 216 JSA Pg. 105 Earl Meshigaud
Pg. 125 Maureen Zarella Pg. 115,126, 145, 204 & 224 Jessie Seronko. Pg.
142 Jesuit Retreat House Lake Winnebago, WI. Pg. 167 Ginny Weiss-
man. Pg. 98 & 230 Pixabay. Pg. 242 Doug Hewitt. Pg. 248 WCPT 820.
"Human Family" 1993 JSA. All Rights Reserved.
"Sweet Surrender" © 1974, and *"Annie's Song"* © 1974 words and music
by John Denver, used by permission. All Rights Reserved.
Front cover image Teresa Rodriguez.
Back cover image Patricia Hardwick.

For my friend, the late, great Richard Crowe, legendary ghost hunter, author, and lecturer, who dedicated his life to teaching how phenomenal life can be, if we pay attention.

AUTHOR'S PREFACE

It's been nine years since I wrote *Every Moment Matters* and thirteen since *Living An Uncommon Life* and while both of them did well on the very crowded "self-help" shelf, crammed next to titles that promise greater success, money, and power, neither of my first two books were designed with that result in mind. I was simply writing about my own life, and while authenticity doesn't grab headlines, it does seem to resonate in a time that on many levels seems so very inauthentic, where the line of reality has become blurred.

So, while I have enjoyed responses from readers around the world about my work, publishing (especially self-publishing and all that goes with it) is not for the faint of heart, and even the greatest authors eventually end up in the same place – the bargain book bin. One time, I found a copy of *Every Moment Matters* in the $1.99 pile next to John Grisham and Anne Lamott, which made me feel really good.

So, why go through this all over again?

I call it, "The Nudge."

In late 2018, there was a very strong, deep, inner pressure to put some of my more "unique" experiences between the covers of a book. Over the years I have learned, to some degree, that if I don't take action when that feeling comes, it gets harder to ignore and tends to create a serious case of spiritual constipation, and the only antidote is to proceed as instructed, even though I don't have the full blueprint.

One of the overriding lessons for me in my life, is that *listening is everything*, and that acting on those inner instructions, *come what may*, is of utmost importance, for reasons that are often unclear in the moment, and sometimes don't show up until years later. All of the experiences, epiphanies, occurrences, visitations, coincidences, and other shit I cannot explain in this book, is based on that understanding. A cosmic game of connect-the-dots is going on all around us, and for the most part, we are too busy to notice, stuck as we are in the constant battle for our attention being waged between the news programming, talk shows, podcasts, blogs, Facebook, Twitter, and Instagram.

So, don't expect any blatant "self-help" stuff in this book because the purpose is more about "inspiration" a.k.a.

"divine influence or action on a person believed to qualify him or her to receive and communicate sacred revelation" which accurately sums all that you are about to read. While I am not anointed in any special way, I do understand that to whom much is given, much is expected; and that *inspiration* can lead to *transformation.*

Before I type one more word on my trusty, dusty, Dell laptop, a disclaimer for you: All that follows is true and to the best of my recollection, although some details, now decades later, are a little fuzzy around the edges. Also, I've omitted names of those people that I couldn't reach for their permission to be included, changed some names to protect those who may not even have known the role they played in the experience, and I offer my thanks those who allowed me to include them as witnesses (for lack of a better term) further validating these events.

And, while I know these experiences impacted me and those who participated in them, it doesn't necessarily mean, even after replaying these events hundreds of times in my head, that I fully understand them, as for the most part, I can only see my piece of the puzzle. It's from that perspective that I share these incredible and extraordinary events, the *phenomena.*

One definition of phenomena is, *"An unusual, extraordinary, unexplained event. Phenomena are often, but not always, understood as 'things that appear' or 'experiences' for a sentient being, or in principle may be so."*

I doubt that anyone who watched me play high school, college or semi-pro football would call me a "sentient being" but I digress.

My only slightly elevated consciousness makes it very difficult to major in minor things. I care far less about sports, politics, and other distractions than I did before the two "near death experiences" I had by the age of 27 and over time I view those simply as platforms for human behavior, where the good, the bad and the ugly are on full display.

I am convinced that we all have a *"sixth insatiable sense"* as my friend songwriter David Stoddard describes it, an extra sensory app that allows us to go past the five basic senses that come as standard equipment at birth, and not just see, taste, smell, feel, and hear, but also *energetically* "experience" the world we live in. But, over time, it gets pushed farther and farther back behind the firewall of our logical mind, and like any other muscle, atrophies if it's not exercised on a regular basis. To that end, in my experience by adjusting my spiritual sight on that which is often overlooked, I have been able to strengthen my ability to not just read between the lines, but to also see the spaces that hold the lines together-and add spaces, that's where the real magic is.

As I began to compile the events of this book, and word spread I often found myself in conversation with friends and family who eagerly began to share with me, their own experiences of *phenomena*, but had been uncomfortable talking about them, for various reasons. I guess they figured that if I was willing to write a book about this stuff, they had permission to share with me their own insights, the whispers, coincidences, visits, and signs they had experienced, and if we pay attention, the reasons for those occurrences, often reveals itself in time.

So, if you are willing to allow the boundaries of your belief system, that tangled mass of downloaded confirmation bias and other assorted tenets and opinions, to be stretched, you will be amazed to discover, as I have, that you are far more than your politics, your religion, your ethnicity, or even your gender.

     With those limiting barriers removed, you can then begin to understand that how you were born, isn't nearly as important as why.

     Every day that you are alive, is like a blank page in the book of life, sitting upon a shelf, waiting to be written by the longing, higher self.

JSA

-1-

SHOCK THERAPY

January 19, 1978, is a date that is literally burned into my memory banks. I had no way of knowing that when I got called into work at Osco Drug, it would be the night that would change the direction of my life, not just physically, but also metaphysically.

Back then I earned $2.65 per hour stacking shelves, waxing floors and changing price tags while wearing a light blue smock coat with my name tag prominently displayed and box cutter in my pocket. Often, my work was regulated to moving around a serious amount of inventory in the basement of the store, like a human forklift. I was 19 years old, basically bulletproof, had unlimited energy, was in great shape from years on the gridiron and the weight room, and had graduated from high school just eight months earlier. I was attending Northeastern Illinois University in Chicago, on a full scholarship, as I was a pretty good football player, (until a knee injury dramatically cut my chances of playing major college ball,) and it was an honor for me to have the opportunity to play for NEIU.

My biggest football accomplishment up to that point was sacking a future NFL quarterback, David Krieg, twice in one game in 1977 against little Milton College, which no longer exists.

I was putting in my time at the drug store while attending school because I was brought up to work. My dad worked, my mom worked, and it was drilled into me that there is a price for everything, nothing in life is free and that effort is all important, no matter your chosen vocation. So, from my first paper route, to making doughnuts, to pumping gas at the full-service Broadway Surf Standard station, to pouring concrete during my summers off in high school, work was just a part of the deal.

Unfortunately, this work ethic didn't exactly translate into good grades in college. I basically did nothing in class, attended every party I was invited to (and some that I wasn't) lived the high life of a full football scholarship, road trips, and all that goes along with it. My grades, four C's and an F, were probably better than I deserved, but didn't come close to meeting my eligibility requirements to keep my full ride intact, so, if I wanted to play football again in the fall of 1978, I had to pay my half of the tuition, about $685, as I recall.

At 9:55 p.m. one of the girls up at the checkout area made the announcement that the store was closing in just five minutes, which was my signal to start grabbing all the cardboard boxes that had been piling up for most of the evening and shoving them into the "Iron Giant," as I called the massive bailing machine which had a huge gaping mouth of a door on the front where the boxes were fed into. Once full, one press of the button on the side of the machine would exert enough pressure to smash the boxes into a pancake. I would repeat the process over and over again, until there was enough in there to make a hay bale of cardboard, which was then wrapped with sturdy wire, rolled out from the big double doors, and into the parking lot for eventual pickup.

I had completed that procedure many times with no problem. However, just a couple days earlier there was something wrong with the button on the side of the machine and one of the managers told the stock guys to just open the breaker box in the back and use the override button until the other one was fixed.

After a few cycles on the machine, the side button predictably failed. I reached around the iron behemoth, my left hand on the door handle and my right hand pushing the override button as previously instructed.

That was the last conscious action I remember.

I recall a very loud humming noise, a vibration of sorts that seemed to roll around in my body. My head was pulled forward and stuck to the side of the machine, my body now making a three-way contact with 460 volts surging through me, from my right hand on the button, to my head, to my left hand on the door. I was being deep fried from the inside out.

Then, a voice in my head, *"I'm dead."*

That was it. Then just…dark. Nothing, no pain, no hum, just an overwhelming smell of burnt skin and bone. I surrendered to it. I had no other thoughts; it was as if my brain had been wiped clean by an electronic eraser on a blackboard.

At some point, the will to live must have taken over, and my right hand finally pulled away from the point of contact on that button, and I ended up on the hard, concrete floor, not breathing.

I woke up to the pharmacist (a guy named Mike, who had been a medic ten years earlier in Vietnam and who just happened to stay late that night,) pounding on my chest. I had no recollection of what had happened to me or where I was at, and the sight of this guy, feverishly beating on my body was another shock all its own.

He was yelling my name over and over again, which brought the rest of the crew running, all girls as I recall, and they began crying and shouting, pointing at the machine, and gagging at the smell in the stockroom.

What a mess.

The metal snap buttons on my favorite shirt and the cross my grandmother had given me had melted to my chest. My wristwatch literally blew up and the eyelets had blown out of my boots.

It turns out those rubber soled construction boots saved my life. According to the OSHA investigation, had I been wearing hard sole shoes it might have been a different story.

The circuit, while formidable, didn't fully "ground" me, so there would be no obituary listing my death as a work-related accident at the age of 19, but my right hand had taken a severe beating. Parts of it had been blown off and stuck to the wall behind the machine. A hole was lasered into my right thumb and you could see right through it. My ring finger and pinkie were melted together, and my fingerprints now had a permanent design change.

My heart had stopped for an undetermined amount of time, but as best as can be figured, I was stuck on that machine for ten to fifteen seconds, not much in everyday life, but as a human conduit for electricity, it's an eternity.

However, despite the looks on the faces of those around me, the stench of the place, the fact I was "Smurf Blue" because I had been so hot, and the incredible headache I had...I was alive.

Meanwhile, as if in some pre-planned move, Chicago Fire Department Ambulance #32 was literally sitting at the stop light, just one block away when they got the call. Mike finally got off my chest when he realized I was now breathing again, and the paramedics took over, starting with cutting my shirt off to attach the heart monitor electrodes.

"Are you going to shock me again?" I asked in a daze, thinking that the wires were connected to a set of paddles somewhere, just like I saw on the television show, Emergency!

A fireman put his hand on my shoulder and said, "Hell no. You've had enough of that for today."

I don't remember the short ride to Swedish Covenant Hospital. What I do remember is the look on my dad's face when he came into the ER. His face was ashen, and he seemed at a loss of what to say to his strapping son, who was splayed out on a table, with my right arm extended and hand soaking in an ice-cold solution of saline. The ER team had already gently removed the metal shirt buttons that had burned into my skin and cut out the gold chain and cross that had scorched my neck. My watch never made it out of the ambulance and my boots smelled like an old catcher's mitt that had been put in a microwave on high, but that was nothing compared to the acrid stench coming off my right hand that was seared with third degree burns, down to the bone in a couple of places.

The ER doc put up a surgical curtain of sorts, across my right shoulder so I couldn't see what they were about to do. One of the first steps, was to detach my right pinkie from my ring finger and then deal with the hole in my thumb. The team debrided the burns, cutting away charred flesh, and pouring antiseptic over my other burns as well. I laid there, watching the heart monitor machine record an erratic up and down movement, as my ticker tried to figure out what the hell had happened. Turns out that the docs were more concerned about my possible internal damage, more than fingers they could simply amputate.

But that's when my dad stepped in.

He was making the case for keeping the digits intact anyway he could, including telling the lead MD that I was a promising piano player and that eventually, time on the black and white keys would be a great therapy down the road.

I've never played the piano in my life, however, my old man was a pretty fair poker player and somehow convinced the team to let me keep my fingers attached to my hand, no matter how bad they looked at the time.

For the next hour or so, I could see my arm reflected in the plastic face shield the doc wore, as he and the nurses set about removing what they could, leaving what they couldn't and finally, wrapping my hand and arm in a high-pressure sleeve, with a big loop on the end, to keep my hand above my heart to reduce swelling. It looked like I stuck my entire arm into a beehive.

Once the ER docs finished with me, I was sent off to the Burn Unit, which was full of people that were far worse off than I was, so the only place they had room for me was on the floor designated for Parkinson's patients. So, in the space of two hours, I went from being the All-American boy, full of piss and vinegar, to a piece of meat that had been left on the grill too long, with a beehive stuck on his hand, that smelled like death.

The days that followed were a blur. I know my mom and dad kept an ongoing vigil, along with my sister and a few visitors that stopped in. The constant sound of the EKG checking to see if my heart was done bouncing around in my chest cavity filled the room. And, how I hated the smell of my hand, now slung in an IV holder, hanging just a foot from my nose.

Eventually, every few hours nurses would come and go, scrubbing away the dead skin off my hands and neck, irrigating the wounds and then loading them up with stuff called "Betadine" that turned my remaining skin an odd brown color. While it sucked having my hand resemble something that got stuck in a meat grinder, (I had a hard time even looking at my digits) and that damn heart monitor was ever present, but I was more than happy to have skilled care at that point, and from a pretty nurse.

The "blessing in disguise" came a couple of days after I was admitted. A familiar face walked in the door of my hospital room, a young lady named Lori who had been one of the managers for the football team my junior year of high school (she was a senior and had graduated a year before me). She was a dietician at the hospital, and I don't know if we would have connected if I was in the burn unit. She was as surprised to see me, as I was to see her.

While we were "catching up" as it were, a nurse came in to take care of my burns once again. The unwrapping process took a few minutes, and finally my claw- like hand was seen by someone besides the docs and assigned nurses. As my caregiver gently shredded dead skin off, there were faint specks of pink underneath in some spots, signs of new life.

When the nurse was done, I was lathered up, tied up, and my hand once again became a beehive, hanging from the IV holder. My friend from high school said, "*You know Augie, you will never really begin to heal, until you start taking ownership of the pain.*" Those words went through me like another electrical shock.

This casually tossed out phrase, has been with me for over forty years. It speaks to not just the physical pain I was in at the time, but every other form of mental, spiritual, and emotional pain that would come my way.

Can't heal it if you don't feel it.

The docs told me straight up that "you are lucky to be alive" and if one of the girls working that night, (someone perhaps half my size) they would have never had the strength to pull off the machine and that would have been the end of them.

After a week in the hospital, I got home, and took charge of my "healing" turning our little bathroom into a pharmacy/surgical outpatient area, with all of the needed medical supplies provided free of charge from Osco Drug. They were extremely nice to me, hoping I wouldn't sue them. OSHA rules took over, when it was all said and done, (and after paying my lawyer) I had enough cash to buy a 1969 Z28 "bumblebee" Camaro, so all good there.

Fortunately, the follow-up skin grafts worked pretty well. The doctors took some of the flesh from the inside crease of my right elbow and fashioned a little patch over the lower part of my right pinkie so it would have some elasticity, as there was nothing but bone there. I don't have any feeling in the top joint of my right thumb, and the burned area where I touched the button, seared a flat spot that looks like an outline of the Loch Ness Monster to me.

I'm truly amazed that with the devastation to my right hand, I am able to type as I do.

****

Surviving that *"accident"* helped me over time to see an event as an *"incident"* changing me from being a *victim* to a *participant*, and looking for the purpose in all things, even those things I don't particularly like or enjoy.

I am convinced beyond a shadow of a doubt, that electrical "incident" changed something in me, a rewiring of my system I suppose, a jump-start to some sort of "ability" that I already had, but wasn't using.

The electricity that coursed through my body had a definite entry point (my right thumb) and many different exit points. Whether or not you actually expire from electrocution, depends mainly on the body's resistance, the amount of current, and duration. There have been many documented cases of humans being hit by lightning or experiencing a severe electrical shock, and coming out of the other side of the event, very different than when they went in.

A month later, on February 19th I was at home in our living room watching television and a huge shiver came over my body, almost like a seizure. I glanced at the clock and it was 10 p.m. the exact time and to the day, as when I was zapped.

I knew then and there that something was up.

Much if not all I have written about in this book, comes from that one night so very long ago. At times, to be able to hear different "channels" than most people do, see things that most people cannot, or simply be aware of that which most of us miss, is both a blessing and a curse.

Most of what I am sharing on these pages, is not in the realm of *ordinary*, as my journey has been filled with truly phenomenal moments, that have allowed me to experience the *extraordinary*. It's not in the range of normal to "know" when someone you haven't spoken to in a year is pregnant and then they call five minutes later and confirm it. It's not normal to take a 1,000-mile roundtrip walk, and then on that journey, end up in a small shop, and without ever having met the people before, suddenly know everything about them. There is nothing ordinary about being hit by a drunk driver broadside two weeks after getting married, and being literally "knocked out of my body" and then once again getting that, "Man you're lucky to be alive," speech for the second time in just seven years.

I've done a bit of digging into this on and off again "ability," to hear that which seems to be on some wavelength that most humans are not tuned in to. *Clairaudience* is the aptitude of ultra-clear hearing. This intuitive ability, akin to a human dog whistle, can manifest in your life during a crisis, or as a result of a life changing event. It's basically the ability to be able to hear on a "spiritual frequency" with great clarity.

While I often feel like a reluctant messenger at times, somewhere I signed up for this, and to that end, I continue on, doing what I can, where I am with what I have, to "deliver the mail"(or messages,) whether or not anyone actually listens or "reads the mail," isn't my business, that's their business.

Since that January night, I've come to appreciate that life, literally hangs by a thread for each and every one of us. There is no guarantee we will be here tomorrow, or even in the next moment or two. My default position on this is that we come in on time, and leave on time, and what we do with our time is about making choices *and* taking chances, as both are equally important.

Without question, I know my first "near death experience" turned out to be the catalyst that would give birth to my insatiable sixth sense, which to me, is that "still small voice" that I often strain to hear above the noise of my ego, but when listened to, always reminds me of John 16:13 -

"But when He, the Spirit of truth, comes, He will guide you into all the truth; for He will not speak on His own initiative, but whatever He hears, He will speak; and He will disclose to you what is to come."

Indeed.

Or, another way to look at it comes from that great philosopher Bullwinkle J. Moose who looked into his crystal ball and uttered *"Eenie meenie chili beanie, the spirits are about to speak!"*

His sidekick Rocky The Flying Squirrel asks, *"Are they friendly spirits?"*

Bullwinkle answers, *"Friendly? Just listen…"*

-2-

TOP DRAWER

The odds of being struck by lightning are 1 in 700,000. The odds of being the victim of a shark attack are 1 in 11.5 million. The odds of winning the Powerball are 1 in 292 million. The odds of being hit on the head by a falling satellite are 1 in 21 trillion, but the big one is that the odds that you were even born, are 1 in 400 trillion.

So, what are the odds, that I would open a desk drawer in an empty classroom, and inside were stapled pieces of paper that would help a complete stranger who was battling cancer?

Incalculable.

In the summer of 1994, I had been doing a bit of consulting work on a sports project with Walter Payton, the late, great Hall of Fame Chicago Bears running back. I was in the office three days a week, getting ready to launch a really incredible lithograph project that would, in part, benefit the Payton Foundation. During one of my days in the office, I happened to notice a colorful flyer sitting on the top of a pile of papers on Walter's assistant's desk.

There was a picture of a slight, dark haired girl and it read, "Fundraiser for Amy." The girl had terminal cancer in the form of a brain tumor and there was a benefit dinner being held to raise money for her family, to offset mounting medical bills. I was drawn in by the image of this little girl, because less than six months earlier, a fundraiser was planned for my family as well, to help with medical bills for my daughter. In the end, we never had to actually go that route, but the similarities were striking.

Three or four times that day I walked past the desk and glanced at the flyer, until I finally grabbed it and the attached invitation and letter. They were asking for an autographed football from "Sweetness" for their silent auction. That was business as usual for Walter; helping children was a priority in his life. What was unusual, was the feeling that came over me while holding those pieces of paper.

I felt deep down that I should attend that dinner for Amy, but as I have way too many times, I resisted the inner voice. My rational mind kicked in, excuses followed and so I figured the best thing to do is just ask Walter to sign the ball and then have his assistant ship it when the time got closer. The event was scheduled for September, and this was July, so there was plenty of time to figure it all out.

I took the flyer to Walter, he agreed to sign a football and then he looked at me and said, "You should probably take the ball there in person."

Hmm.

I called Teri, the chairperson of the event, and told her who I was and why I was calling. She was overjoyed! To get a response from Walter Payton was more than she had expected! Over the next month or so, we spoke on the phone a few times, and I learned more about Amy's challenges.

She was a healthy little girl until the age of eight, when she began to experience severe headaches, and after getting tested at a Chicago hospital, it was determined that Amy had malignant brain stem tumors. The specialists operated, removed what they could, but there was little hope for her survival, and she was sent home to be comfortable and spend as much time with her family as possible until she took her last breath.

At some point, Amy's family was connected to the angels at St. Jude Children's Hospital in Memphis, the healing center founded by Danny Thomas and known around the world for their work in treating childhood cancer. Amy began radiation therapy for the remaining tumors on her brain stem and spinal cord, but again, hopes for her long term, were not good, she was still considered terminal.

A few weeks before the event, I spoke for the first time with Amy's mother Sue, and I'm sure I stammered a bit as there are no words that I could possibly come up with that would ease her pain. We connected as parents of children who were both facing serious health challenges, helpless on some level to do much about it. When she found out that I did a lot of public speaking, she asked if I would come to the event and meet Amy.

Walter's words rang in my ears.

I accepted the invite, and when I hung up the phone a warm sensation came over me, a bit like a light summer rain, and with it the underlying feeling of *"have no fear about this girl's condition."*

While that was a comforting thought, it was also very strange. Why would I have a good feeling about a little girl I'd never met, and based on everything I had heard, would most likely not be alive by Christmas?

****

Late August rolled around and I ended up on the stage of the Aspen Music Tent in Colorado speaking at the Windstar Foundation's "Choices for the Future" symposium. The symposium was an extension of the think tank founded by the late John Denver and Tom Crum and this annual event featured speakers such as Leo Buscaglia, Barbara Marx-Hubbard, Dennis Weaver, David Brower, and Buckminster Fuller. In 1993, I began working as a full-time cadre substitute and was teaching at my alma mater, Carl Schurz High School, when I got a flyer in the mail for the upcoming 1994 event titled, "The Human Family." At some point in that day, words started to "download" and when I got home from work that afternoon, I sat in the back yard with a piece of paper and wrote a poem titled *Human Family* in less than five minutes.

Little did I know that in 1994, just a couple weeks before the symposium, that my phone would ring while I was cleaning the cat box, and John Denver's office would be on the other end of the line. Dr. Mae Jemison, America's first African American female astronaut had to cancel her appearance, and JD wanted to know if I would fill in.

Lemme check my schedule yes, *I can do that.*

So, on a bright sun-drenched Saturday morning, nestled in the Rockies in Aspen, I finished my talk with the words that had come to me a full year earlier, words that I had embedded in my brain a thousand times, not knowing at the time, where or when they would be shared. A standing ovation confirmed that all was in order, and the fuse had been lit in me in a big way.

****

Then soon enough, it was the night of Amy's event, I arrived about an hour early, and when I entered the banquet hall, I was immediately drawn to a very large framed picture of Amy in her communion dress. It looked like there were two huge wings behind her, a trick of the lighting I said to myself.

As I made my way around the many tables that were filled with donations, I had a deep sense that something else was going on here, beyond the event itself.

Then, suddenly, the room felt like a giant vacuum had sucked all the air out, and that overwhelming feeling washed over me again, *"It's going to be alright..."*

A few moments later Sue and Teri came out, they were about as excited as they could be, for an event like this. I handed over the autographed football from Walter, they added it to a slew of other items for the silent auction, and soon the room was filled to capacity with family, friends, well-wishers, and a gentleman from St. Jude named Dick Shadyac, who I eventually sat next to at the front table.

About midway through dinner, I happened to glance at the little event booklet to read about some of the VIP attendees I was sharing the table with, each of them were incredible people that had made a huge difference in Amy's life, including Mr. Shadyac, who was a close friend of Danny Thomas and helped stabilize St. Jude after the famed actor and humanitarian died in 1991.

While serving as CEO, Dick was honored with the Ellis Island Medal of Honor for exceptional humanitarian efforts and outstanding contributions to the United States. Prior to taking the job as CEO, he was a trial lawyer for the Department of Justice and then an attorney in a successful private practice for over forty years in the Washington D.C. area.

Then, on the next page was my short bio, which paled in comparison to the heavy hitter I was sitting next to. My radio career was still three years in the future, the author tag and publishing contract, twelve years down the line. I had a serious *"what in the world am I doing here besides delivering a football?"* moment.

I turned the page and there it was, for the first time in print, the words to my poem, *Human Family*. I'd forgotten that I included it in the info sent to Teri back in July. I'd never seen it in print, only in my own scribbled handwriting.

So, when it was my turn to speak, I talked about being honored to stand in on behalf of "Sweetness" and the challenging circumstances and events that brought a roomful of strangers and friends, from all backgrounds, colors, creeds, and beliefs together, and the common denominator being a little eight-year-old girl who was fighting for her life.

Then, something inside me clicked, and in that moment, I was having some sort of out-of-body experience, as I realized that no one in the room was moving, the wait staff was standing still listening, no glasses tinkling, or small talk in the back of the room. I was nothing more than a conduit of some higher consciousness where the messenger becomes far less important than the message being delivered, in this case, it would be a simple poem.

As I concluded, I began to share the words of that poem they all held before them on the event program, and about half way through, I realized that Dick Shadyac was quietly reading out loud along with me, the healing energy in the room was palpable, as other voices joined in, just above a whisper, almost prayer-like.

What a powerful, humbling experience.

A bit later, Amy finally came to the podium. She had been too weak to attend the whole event and had been listening and resting in another room. As her dad John helped her to the microphone that feeling of a "blessed assurance" about Amy's condition came over me again, like a blanket of peace.

She spoke quietly and slowly, choosing her words carefully, as if there was someone whispering in her ear, telling us what we all needed to hear. When she finished, her father led her back towards the little side room as we all stood in silence watching this frail little girl fighting for her life.

I drove home totally spent.

****

Just a couple of days or so after Amy's event, I was doing the substitute teaching thing at Schurz and was assigned to cover an English class on the 2nd floor, right down the hall from the lunchroom. Perfect, I could pontificate about Steinbeck for forty minutes, then be in the teacher's lounge with a full tray of chow and find a good seat before it got crowded. I arrived at the room five minutes before the bell, opened the door, turned on the lights, and stood at the entrance waiting to greet thirty-five high school juniors.

It quickly became clear that word had spread about the regular teacher being absent, and that gave the kids permission to bug out. Not one of them showed up. Since I was assigned to the room, I grabbed a newspaper, put my feet up on the desk and read it cover to cover. That burned up about fifteen minutes, and I had another thirty minutes to go. So, I did what most subs do, started rummaging around in the desk for any sort of food product that might be stashed. I was striking out (it's usually the bottom right-hand drawer) and there was only one more drawer, the top left.

I yanked it open and sitting on top of a few books were six or eight pages of an article stapled together with the title highlighted in yellow, *"Keeping Hope Alive."* I started to read the article that was about treating and curing cancers with herbal treatments. The focus was on a product that was invented by Canadian nurse named Rene Cassie back in the early 1920's. I read the story quickly and when I got to the fourth page, there was one line that was also highlighted like the title, and flashed like a neon sign in my mind.

"Effective against brain tumors and especially brain stem tumors."

No way.

I read the rest of the article, and as if by some pre-arranged agreement, went over to the copier in the corner of the room, and copied the article, putting the original back in the drawer, and highlighting the copy just like the original.

The rest of the day was a bit of a blur as I began to wrestle with and try to comprehend the information that had just "shown up" in an empty classroom, that might be of value to Amy and her family.

That night when I got home, just before I went to bed, I did something very much out of the ordinary for me. I literally got down on my knees and asked for guidance. What if this stuff was fake? What if it didn't work? What if I called Sue and John, and told them about what I found, and got their hopes up? Would they take information from a near stranger? On and on I argued with myself, a tug of war that seemed to have no right answer. Then, the thought came to contact Teri, for her opinion.

When I shared with her what had taken place, she insisted that I should hang up with her immediately, call Sue and John, so I did.

I must have sounded like a rambling idiot, trying to put into words the feelings I had at the event, covering a class with no kids in the room, then finding the stapled papers with the highlighted words, all the while apologizing because I know that when a child is up against it, people come out of the woodwork with all sorts of information and it can be overwhelming.

Sue was very quiet during the call, and then finally she said that I needed to know that the very time that I was on my knees, so were she and John, feverishly praying for something, anything that might help Amy.

Wow. While, I was coming up with excuses not to call, they were praying for a reason that someone would.

I mailed the article to Sue and I thought it best to just leave it be. A few weeks later, she called to say that they had added the herbals to Amy's protocol, as she was in such a grave condition it couldn't make anything worse. Amy was having a bit of a time getting the tea down, but they were determined to stay with it.

Nearly a year passed with no word and I would often check the obituary pages just in case. Then one night the phone rang. It was Sue, she was crying so hard I could hardly understand her words, finally she took a deep breath and told me that Amy had gone for a check-up at St. Jude and the results were unbelievable! What was left of her brain tumor was gone! In addition, the tumors on her spine had shrunk significantly! I was dumbfounded, awestruck, and humbled all at the same time.

****

Fast forward to 2019.

The little eight-year-old girl, who was given just months to live, recently celebrated her 33rd birthday. While she has endured 19 brain surgeries, a stroke, and numerous setbacks, she remains an upbeat, optimistic, incredible young woman.

Amy has had more challenges in the past twenty-five years than most people have in an entire lifetime. Her presence, in and of itself, is a testament to the indomitable human spirit that resides in all of us, but mostly remains hidden underneath the layers of life, until we are tested.

I reached out and connected with Sue as I wrote this chapter, talking for the better part of an hour, recapping and recounting, confirming, and qualifying all the events for accuracy. She is staunch in her belief, that while these years have been unbelievably difficult for their family, this is Amy's journey and while she still battles daily with pain, she anoints all whom she connects with. She maintains that back in 1994, that herbal tea, combined with a deep, knowing faith and the ongoing commitment from the incredible people of St. Jude, has made all the difference.

We spoke of the puzzle pieces of life, strewn about when we are faced with our own mortality, or that of a loved one, especially a child. Priorities rearrange, what matters most comes forth, our troops circle the wagons, and the precious gift of being alive becomes front and center, something that we usually don't acknowledge when life seems to be at its most mundane.

Wake-up calls are there for a reasons and seasons, and sometimes both. For me, the overarching "lesson" (for lack of a better term) from this experience, is about giving *attention* to your *intention*. There was a deep desire in me to somehow be of assistance to Amy and her family, connected on some level to my daughter, who also had a serious health condition. And, in ways that are past my knowing and understanding, all of these events lined up to help that deep desire be fulfilled. Following the connect-a-dots, it becomes clear that the nuances, nudges, and nods that were hidden on the path emerged and revealed that which I was seeking; and in fact, was seeking me. The answers were "in here" before I ever found them in that desk drawer in an empty classroom

Arguing with my ego has always been a tug-of-war, as the "false self" doesn't recognize a power greater than its own wounds, fears, darkness, and denial. Time and time again, my ego has been spiritually pounded into submission, after it has run out of options and supposed answers, and then…the amazing chain of events beginning with a flyer on the desk and all the way to finding six stapled pieces of paper - the exact information needed at just the right time.

All of that and more, is beyond my capability to orchestrate, and while just a small piece in the mosaic of Amy's life, it's verifiable proof that if you pay attention, the next drawer you open, might hold the answers to the some of the biggest questions in your life.

I've edited, re-worded, and quadrupled checked this chapter more than any other in this book, making sure that I find the words that accurately convey how remarkable and "sacred" this experience was (and continues to be) for me, as it resonated with the energy of a greater force, of spirit, of healing.

It has become apparent to me, that the Architect of the Universe has a blueprint for each of us, that if followed, might not ever be easy, but certainly can be truly and utterly phenomenal, and create a ripple effect that can last for decades.

-Human Family-

Have you ever sat in wonder at the setting of the sun?

Or how a flower blossoms and that summer always comes?

Ever held a snowflake or dried a small child's tears?

Ever dreamed of peace and love, throughout your living years?

You're the heart of the Human Family, the promise of life to come, the pulse of the living world, you are the only one.

Have you ever walked in the rain, and smelled the sweetness of drops in the wind? Ever knelt in humble prayer in forgiveness of imagined sin?

Have you ever hurt so bad that you swear you would rather die?

Then, woke the next morning to see rainbows in the sky?

You're the eyes of the Human Family, the promise of life to come, a prophet of faith and giver of dreams, you are the only one.

Have you ever seen the hunger, in the children of the land?

And watched as we consume ourselves, destroying what we don't understand?

Ever stood in silence, as the leaders slowly take their fall?

Prayed for their legacy and all the names on cold stone walls?

You're the voice of the Human Family, the promise of life to come, singer of songs for all the world and your greatest has yet to be sung.

On this day sit in wonder at the miracle you truly are. Know that your light shines from the heavens within and is as bright as a midnight star.

Dream of a world without hunger, where the children never shed cruel tears.

Know that we can make that happen, by living through untrue fears.

We are the Human Family, with footsteps in the sand.

We are the Human Family, walking hand in hand.

We are the Human Family, responsible for all we see.

We are the Human Family; the truth will set you free.

-3-

THE CHIEF

I have come to the conclusion based on some of the experiences recounted in this book (and a few others I still have kept to myself,) that it's totally possible that when we die, an unseen part of us lives on, so that connections can be made with those who still are alive for reasons that might not show themselves for many years. The ripple effect of these "connections" can have far ranging effects that are often not recognized in the actual moment they take place.

While that might sound like some farfetched new-age psychic medium drivel, I have had too many experiences that fall into the category of "believe it or not" and while they often leave me with more questions than answers, each experience opened doors of potential enlightenment and growth, I could not imagine in the moment.

Such are the encounters I had with a Native American chief who died 86 years before I was born. My path to this encounter was a tortuous route, starting with a near fatal auto accident in May 1986 when the car I was driving was hit broadside, by an intoxicated guy in a speeding Cadillac that started a chain reaction of change, none of it easy, or invited, but on some level, part of a bigger plan.

At least that's how I have come to understand and interpret all that follows.

While I survived the collision physically that night, weeks later after sitting in a hot courtroom watching the man that nearly killed me get off with a slap on the wrist – a mere $100 fine for running a red light – the volcano erupted on a serious case of PTSD that had been boiling under the surface, like a river of lava. A series of panic attacks had me locked down for a few days in Sheridan Road Hospital in Chicago, unable to control the anger, energy, and emotions that were flooding my central nervous system. For someone who felt pretty much like Superman most of my life, this inner Kryptonite was contaminating my belief system and chipping away at me, breaking me into little pieces and there wasn't anything I could do about it, until I began to understand what was happening.

When the doctors finally figured out that there was a lot of unresolved emotion around some major life events, that accident (while devasting on many levels on its own) was the tipping point in my life in a big way. Once they diagnosed that I wasn't a candidate for *One Flew Over the Cuckoo's Nest*, I was sent home with an ongoing prescription for Xanax and told that in time the PTSD would simply resolve itself.

Bullshit.

The smallest infraction would set me off, anything that came into the peripheral vision of my left eye, a bird, bug or sudden movement, had me in a core meltdown. The instructions were that when I felt "anxious" I should take a couple of the horse pill sized sedatives and eventually it would "calm me down." So, for a time, I rode a teeter-totter of being "The Hulk" when something tripped my trigger and his much calmer alter ego Dr. David Banner, after knocking back the Xanax.

Adding those drugs to my already amped up personality? Not a good combo.

When I found out the side effects included paranoid or suicidal thoughts and impaired memory, judgment, and coordination, I knew that this was not a long-term solution. So, I decided to drop the pills and work my way through it from *the inside out,* dealing with the overwhelming feelings of anger and pain, in a more constructive way.

For whatever reason, the movie *Back to the Future* became an anchor for me. I would pull the mattress off the box spring, drag it into the living room, put the VHS tape of the movie on, and watch it until I fell asleep. I performed this nocturnal routine, every single night for an entire year.

During that time, I learned to do mental exercises when I felt that "energy" coming over me, in that I would picture a metal bar in my mind, and then bend and unbend it until the feeling passed. I made more pretzels of out of iron, that only I could see, than could easily be counted. I started to understand the mind/body connection at a level I never thought of before, all brought on by a drunk driver.

The car accident was a veiled invitation to change directions. I quit my job, decided to go back to college and ended up working overnight at the long-gone Ramada Hotel O'Hare (a book in itself) as a security officer on the 3rd shift. Being active for eight hours when most of the world was asleep, had a somewhat calming effect on me as well (except for throwing drunks out of the bar). There was a lot of property to be covered, and I walked off my PTSD in chunks, making the rounds, checking on doors, grabbing menus, surveying the grounds as needed.

That also meant that my sleep pattern was different, and that helped a great deal. I learned to take serious naps during the day, readjusting my mind and "switching gears" as it were, between working, attending college, and beginning to raise a family. At night, usually around 3 a.m. I would go to the very top of "The Tower" where the elegant banquet hall was located, then climb a set of iron steps up to the roof and sit for a long time, overlooking O'Hare airport to the west and the lights of Chicago to the east, from twelve stories up.

At some point in all this transition, I began to take long walks in the forest preserve just two blocks away from the apartment, usually during the early morning after I got off my shift. I've always loved the woods and had spent many hours camping and making my way through any forest I could find. This one particular day I crossed East River Road and made my way south, through a dense growth of trees, then across a broad expanse of prairie grass and then through another, sparser tree line.

When I emerged into a clearing, there sat a massive boulder with a bench on each side of it. I walked around to the front of the formidable chunk of stone and read the words carved on it…

What a discovery! How many other people knew of this stone?! What is this place that I had stumbled across in the heart of the wilderness? I was ready to stake a claim on this hallowed ground…until the faint noise of traffic caught my ear, and slightly disappointed, I realized that this might not be as remote a location as I thought.

One glance to my left had me stowing my Lewis & Clark attitude, as there was an asphalt path leading from a small parking area on the main road, with a fence around it that lead to where I was standing. Cars were whizzing by, oblivious to my presence. I spied a sign that was posted near the entrance of the place. There was a grainy picture of a man with his hair styled in the manner of a time long past, wearing a heavy frock like coat and frilly tie, with formidable shoulders and intent, squinting gaze.

The image was a bit unsettling for me, and I wasn't sure why.

The information posted on the sign, indicated that Alexander Robinson was born on Mackinac Island and was indeed of mixed race of British and Ottawa heritage. His name (*Chee-Chee-Pin-Quay*) translates to "Squinting eye" and its possible he might have had some sort of tick or affliction with his sight.

He became a fur trader and ultimately settled near what later became Chicago. He spoke three languages Odawa, Potawatomi, Ojibwa (or Chippewa) as well as English and French, and Robinson also helped evacuate survivors of the Fort Dearborn Massacre in 1812. In 1816, Robinson was a translator for native peoples during the Treaty of St. Louis. He became a Potawatomi chief in 1829 and then in 1833, he and Billy Caldwell (who was also known as Sauganash) negotiated treaties on behalf of the United Nations of Ottawa, Chippewa, and Potawatomi with the United States. In reward for his efforts in obtaining the 1829 treaty, the U.S. granted Robinson $200 annually and a 1600-acre tract of land, known as the Robinson Reserve, along the Des Plaines River (that was adjacent to land given Caldwell on the North Branch of the Chicago River.) By 1840, Alexander Robinson returned to the Chicago area, although he would later make treks to Kansas and in 1845, he built a house on the Robinson Reserve and on April 22, 1872, he passed away at the age of 85. The original headstones of the Robinson family had been vandalized and lost for a time, hence the common marker that designated the burial ground for Robinson and his family. Matter of fact, the original grave marker for Robinson had his age at 110 years when he passed.

I could have easily driven the ¾ of a mile route from my apartment to the parking lot, and walked in as most people did, but for some reason, I had to make my way through the forest, a more traditional path of sorts, following in the footsteps of Robinson and his family, without even knowing it.

I spent many a morning with "The Chief" sitting for long periods of time, after my shift at the hotel, unwinding, watching deer, listening to birds greet the day, and keeping track of the "gifts" visitors were compelled to leave on or near the stone. There was a constant offering of copper pennies, small stones, pinches of tobacco, sage, flowers, sweetgrass, and feathers.

So, when the opportunity came for me to get out of the overnight security gig and put my years of weightlifting and fitness to use as a personal trainer at a health club near the apartment, I jumped at the chance.

About six months after I started, my manager referred a client to me who was recovering from a lower back injury. Ann had been instructed to continue with her PT (physical therapy) by getting at PT (personal trainer) and I was the choice. She was diligent in her training but around the third session, the conversation went from *the physical*, to *the metaphysical*.

Not sure what prompted it, but Ann started talking about finding pennies in the oddest places, and that she had a certain "ability" to discern that which most of us miss. I didn't say much (for a lot of clients their personal trainers are half psychologists as well) and I just let her ramble, while urging her to pick up the pace on the treadmill.

When she finished, Ann went to the locker room to get changed, but hesitated before going in. "You know, it's not a coincidence that you are my trainer. When the time is right, perhaps you will trust me enough to take me to that place you spend so much time at, you know…where those pennies are."

My mouth was hanging open like a trout out of water gasping for air.

During the next nine sessions the subject never came up again, even though I thought about it every time she had an appointment. How in the hell could she have possibly known?

Ann did well with her training and that was that, pretty much case closed. Or so I thought.

One day in late October of 1990, a couple of months after Ann had completed her training, I got a call from the front desk in the training office. I had a visitor, but they didn't give their name. So, I went up front, and there stood Ann, big smile on her face and said she couldn't stay long but wanted to drop something off for me.

Uh…*okay*.

"Close your eyes and stick out your hand."

I did.

When I opened my eyes, there was a well-worn copper penny, with "ONE CENT" tacked on it.

Okay…so that's uh…great…and…?

"Turn it over" she said.

There on the front, was what appeared to be a man wearing a headdress of feathers. I'd never actually held an Indian Head penny before.

"He's a chief, like the man that you visit all the time."

What the…*what*?

I pulled her off to the side, away from the ears of the girls at the front desk.

"Listen, thank you so much for this. But seriously, how do you know what you know about me and that place I spend so much time at?"

"I told you that I have a gift, ever since I was little. Just the way it is. I don't tell everyone, just people that need to know, and then I am like a 'connector' for the two sides of spirit."

"Two sides of spirit?"

"Yes, here…*and there*. Two sides, one spirit."

She made it sound so simple, but it was a foreign language to me, even with some of the more "beyond belief" experiences I had up to that point. This was a direct and intended contact made by someone who felt they were being "guided" in my direction, for what exactly I didn't know.

There we sat on a couch in the lobby of a very busy health club, Ann doing most of the talking, and me trying to understand just a little of what she was attempting to share with me. To the staff, it looked like I was chatting with a client, but the opposite was true, I was sitting with a teacher of sorts, a communicator who had gotten her ego out of the way and was willing to be a conduit. Finally, she said that perhaps before the weather got too cold, she would meet me at "the place" and then fulfill her spiritual obligation, whatever that might be.

I reluctantly agreed.

We decided to meet two days later, on a Thursday evening, around 5:30 p.m.

I gave her the directions and she said, "no offense but I kind of already know where it is."

Huh.

I got to the Robinson Burial Grounds at 5 p.m. a full 30 minutes early, just to sit and absorb the place. As the autumn afternoon light began to fade, a car pulled up behind mine in the parking area. Ann got out, started to walk into the front entrance when she abruptly stopped.

She just stood there.

After probably five minutes (seemed a lot longer) she finally made her way in, acknowledged me sitting on the bench that is on south side of the walkway, went directly to the massive stone monument and once again, just stood there, arms folded, eyes closed.

A light rain began to fall, I shuddered a bit as the wind came up and after what seemed like hours, Ann finally stepped back and sat down across from me, on the bench in the north direction.

"I had to first ask permission to enter this place. Then, I asked permission to help you get the messages you need from this man."

"Okay."

"Do you know that he waits for you every single day? He anticipates you coming here and spending time. He stands on this spot…just waiting…"

Then, she rose to her feet.

"He stands like this" and she once again crossed her arms across her chest, elbows near her waist, hands up towards her shoulders. "There is a woman that stands behind him, she isn't connected to you, but she is very important to him."

I had nothing to say, so Ann continued.

"You have to understand I will not come back to this place again after tonight. So, if you have questions, now is the time."

It only took a few seconds for me to respond, the questions flooded forth.

"Why me? Are we related or something? Why does it matter if I come here or not? Why does he wait for me like that? Who is he?"

She stepped to the northern edge of the stone, put her hand on it and said, *"You are not blood of my blood, but you have been my son for many moons."*

"What...does...that...mean?"

"When you were a small boy, living far from this place near the river, you stopped and picked up a stone and put it in your pocket. Later, you threw that stone into the river and sent forth a ripple that went back into the time I was here, and then forward to this time now. That's why you are drawn to this place. The stone is the stone is the stone."

"I don't understand any of that."

"It's not important anymore, but you asked."

"Why does he wait for me then?"

"Because of how you walked here, across the grass, the old way, from the north to the south."

"Who is he?"

"He is the man who is buried here. Robin's Son."

"Robinson?"

"Yes, but he pronounces it '*Robin's Son.*' This is his land. Many people come here, but few of them listen. You take the time to listen. It means a great deal to him."

"I listen but apparently I don't hear very well."

"True. The only reason I am here is because you cannot hear him. You *feel* him when he is near, and now it's time that you heard what he wants you to *hear.*"

"Hear what?"

"We have to go where he is buried."

"I thought we were already at his burial site."

Ann started walking to the south, about 20 yards or so, and put her hands on a tree, one that looked different than the rest of the oak and maple broadleaf.

"He's buried here" she said, and with that I realized that we were standing by a gnarled Scots Pine. "This is part of his heritage. This is where he is buried."

I scanned the burial site area in the fading light, and there were no other trees like it to be seen. In all the time I had spent there, I'd never noticed it.

Then, all of a sudden, she said, "WAIT FOR IT…WAIT FOR IT…"

Wait for what? I had a fleeting thought that this is when the curtain gets pulled back and I was on some hidden camera show or something. Just then the ground began to shake, a low rumble that grew in magnitude until a deafening roar filled the forest.

It was a jet plane descending for landing at O'Hare, not 500 feet above the tree line. The roar of the engines made it impossible to continue talking. We both just stood there as the big plane continued west towards the airport, and after it cleared the area, a strong rush of wind that had been pulled along by the big bird, washed over the forest in a very loud wave, pulling the treetops along with it.

A few moments passed then Ann said, "He doesn't understand what all that noise is. He witnessed so much during his time on earth, but the noise makes him tremble, every single time."

She knelt down next to the tree as the light rain continued to fall.

The smell of the woods, the damp earth and the sounds of the forest were coming back into focus, after the assault of the giant airliner and the fumes from jet fuel that still lingered in the air.

"This is how it's supposed to be; this is how he remembers it. It's one of the reasons you come here, you need to know this."

"My God what are we doing?" I blurted out.

I wasn't referring to the experience I was having at the burial ground, but rather to the impact humans have on every corner of the planet, much of it without a conscious thought to the consequences of our actions.

"This is how it's supposed to be," she repeated.

We sat by that tree for a long time, and she shared other thoughts about why I was drawn to that place, at that time. Much of it I have forgotten, but as we were about to leave, she said something that has stayed with me all these years.

"As I said when I arrived, this is my first and last time here. I will not come back. I am merely an interpreter, and in some sense that is what you are being asked to do. Interpret the natural world and translate it to people in a way they can understand and connect to the earth. You are to wear this place as if it was an amulet around your neck. You cannot bring everyone here, but you can bring the energy of this place to everyone you come in contact with.

When the time comes for you to die, a part of you will always be here."

In that moment, I didn't have a problem with her words, matter of fact, I felt honored, and still do.

****

About a year later, I was driving to my friend Gary's house on a rainy late summer evening just to hang out. I had Steve Miller blasting on the car stereo, the windows down despite the rain and was driving on Dee Road, just past Maine South High School and clearly remember just making it through the light before it turned red.

Not ten seconds later, suddenly and without warning, *there was a man standing in the middle of the road*! He flashed before my eyes like a scene from a movie. He was fairly tall, with some sort of old-world clothing, wearing a ceremonial headdress of sorts, but not looking fully like a Native American. He was facing me, standing firm and his right arm was straight out, pointing to the east.

HOLY SHIT! I hit my brakes and skidded a bit… I swerved around the man so I wouldn't hit him and instantly looked in the mirror and these words came to my mind and out of my mouth, ***"DON'T EVER FORGET."***

Then in a flash, he was gone. There was nothing in the mirror, but darkness.

Overcome with emotion, confusion, nausea, and a measured bit of fear, I pulled over to the side of the road and marked the spot as there were seven pine trees planted in the parkway, across from the forest preserve to the east.

I forgot all about going to Gary's and sped over to my friend Dan's house, as I needed to share what had happened. I was sure glad he that he was home because I was a wreck at the door, trying to explain to him what had taken place, less than ten minutes earlier.

He listened, and then said we should drive back over there, to that spot, to those pine trees.

I dropped a couple of F-bombs and said that there was no way in hell I was driving on that section of road ever again if I could help it.

After a short discussion, I agreed to go back.

Dan and I drove to the very spot I saw the man, right near a big clearing in the woods to the east and by those pine trees to the west. Dan pulled out some tobacco and did a blessing for that place and what had transpired.

I didn't say much at all. I know what I saw, and that was enough.

It wasn't until the next day that I realized that road was the northern boundary of the land given to Alexander Robinson in the treaty of Prairie du Chien back in 1829, and that part of the reserve was named for his wife, Catherine Chevalier.

****

Not long ago, I was back at the 'Robin's Son' land, it was very quiet, except for a deer, that came up within two feet of me, looking for food. I just sat there on the same bench, thinking about all the incredible experiences I'd had there over the years, too many to mention in just one chapter.

The deer stayed for a very long time, I thanked it for coming to spend a few moments with me and put down some tobacco and seven pennies on the headstone.

Just as I was leaving, the ground began to shake, as another plane filled with people began its descent into O'Hare. I just stood there, waiting for the shaking to stop, listening for the rush of the tailwind that followed and then went back, put down another pinch of tobacco and went on my way.

That burial ground has played an important role in my life, as it pertains to the "mission" that I've accepted, and the message I learned there, one that I have often faltered on, but never wavered from. Those "visits" were the catalyst for much of the environmental work I've done in the media for the past two decades, most especially the "Earth Matters" radio series

We have the responsibility to live in a way that considers the next seven generations to follow. In order to do that, there are five very important things that we must keep in mind.

First, there is the Earth itself, the heart of which is molten liquid metal at the center but allows life to thrive at the temperate surface. All the rocks, stones, mountains and canyons that make up the bones of earth. *Second,* there is the plant life and crops, which includes all that grows from the roots up, from a single weed poking through a crack in the concrete to the mighty Sequoia. *Third,* is the non-human animal life, all that swims, crawls, walks and flies. From the great whales to the ant in your backyard. *Fourth,* is the atmosphere of oxygen that encompasses Earth and protects all life by creating just the right pressure that allows liquid water to exist, all the oceans, seas, lakes, rivers, streams, and ponds.

Fifth, and final piece of this incredible puzzle is the deadliest species on earth, *humans.*

None of the other four components need us to survive. But without them, we are up shit creek without a paddle. If any of the other four are out of balance, we are ensuring that we put ourselves and future generations on the endangered species list.

While I can't say for sure who it was standing in the middle of road that night, on my end, it's totally possible that "The Chief" was making an appearance. However, not all connections are made with the eyes, sometimes it's the spirit that matters more.

I am not alone when it comes to "encounters" at the Robinson Family Burial Grounds. For many years, various "phenomena" has been experienced by visitors at several locations at or near the burial site, orbs of light have been spotted after dark, dancing back and forth on the many trails that zigzag across the area.

Perhaps it's Alexander Robinson inviting those who will listen, to see how life is supposed to be.

Alexander Robinson (Chee-Chee-Pin-Quay)

-4-

TIRE TRACKS

I have a list of events in my mind, that are so far beyond the realm of my consciousness when they happened, pushed the limits of my sanity, and had I not participated in, had witnesses and a time line to hold them together, I wouldn't believe they ever actually took place.

At the top of that list, is "The Jesus Man" an incredible healing I experienced and that I wrote about in my second book, *Every Moment Matters*.

In the #2 slot, would be the event you are about to read.

While all that follows is true, I have changed certain names, and omitted others, due to the fact that I didn't feel that reaching out after all these years was in anyone's best interest and might be an uncomfortable situation for all involved, especially me, even though 27 years have passed, this is still difficult for me to share on many levels.

Back in 1992, I was working with a former NFL player. He was an extremely popular trainer, due to his pro sports background, a very knowledgeable guy, and always looking for ways to improve performance for his clients. At some point, he had developed a small magazine geared towards professional athletes and I was intrigued by the idea of "insider information" for a very select demographic. We eventually partnered up and built the thing from a twelve-page newsletter type deal into a fairly successful thirty- two-page, four color offering with tips and information on everything from finances to vacations, training and interviews, all geared towards a readership of about 5,000 pro athletes around the world at that time.

Small demographic, but with an average income of about $3.5 million dollars, it was an elite group that we could secure higher end advertising for and we did just that.

In the fall of that year, I decided that a trek west to Colorado was in order, it was not only a chance for my family to take a serious road trip, but also to use the magazine as leverage to upgrade from staying in a KOA Campground, to four-star resort in the Aspen area. I had made a deal that gave us a week at the resort, in exchange for writing a review in an upcoming issue of the magazine. I had also traded out ad space for a brand-new Ford Explorer, so we had plenty of room to stuff all the needed elements that a family of four required to drive the 1,167 miles from Chicago to Aspen.

The trip coincided with an annual symposium held by the Windstar Foundation in the Aspen Music Tent called, "Choices for the Future" (that you read about in Chapter 2) which was created by the vision of internationally known singer/songwriter and conservationist John Denver and his longtime friend Tom Crum. JD and Tom had created Windstar in 1976 and then in 1978 John purchased 985 acres of land in Old Snowmass, then donated the land to Windstar for various workshops, events, and activities. The foundation was based on making conscious choices that would lead to sustainable practices on many levels. My former wife and I had been there in 1989 and we decided that since our daughter was almost four and son going on two, the drive would be uneventful, and a week in the Rockies a great experience.

Uneventful? Nothing could have been further from the truth.

The day before we left on the trip, my son Andy went in for a checkup. He was a sturdy little man, and we were given the thumbs-up regarding hauling the 18-month old half-way across the country, and confident that his sister would keep tabs on him in the back seat of the truck.

I had already packed the Explorer the night before, so we bugged out around 2 a.m. the next morning and it was off to the races, southbound from Chicago straight through Illinois and then towards Missouri, with a hard right towards Kansas and eventually Colorado.

The first day was fine; made it all the way through to Kansas City and found a place to grab some dinner and sleep for a while, before heading to the Rockies. I woke up early that next morning, while everyone was still sleeping in the truck, bugged out before the sun came up.

At some point, it was light enough to see into the back seat, Andy was on the passenger side, still sleeping in his car seat, but I noticed with a glance in the mirror, that something was hanging off his left ear. Didn't think much of it and kept going, racking up the miles and eventually we stopped for gas.

That's when we knew something was definitely not right with him. His color was okay, but skin was starting to shed off of his hands and face, and his bright blue eyes looked bloodshot. No fever, maybe he just needed water or something, can't be anything seriously wrong, he just had a checkup. So, we made him comfortable and kept going west.

We drove all day until we made it just outside of Sterling, Colorado where we saw a sign for a medical center. By now, Andy was really looking like he had been left out in the sun too long. Sitting for hours didn't help, and we figured better safe than sorry. We pulled into the ER, explained the situation and after a thorough exam, they had no answer as to why this was happening. The doctor said, "Internally he's fine, but there is something else going on."

No shit Sherlock.

It's a solid two-hour drive from Sterling to Denver, so I hit it hard, made it in about 90 minutes and we checked into a downtown hotel, filled the tub with cool water, as his skin was getting more and more red. We stood him up, and washed him down, letting the water run from the top of his head to his toes.

He screamed at the top of his little lungs the whole time. As a parent, there's nothing worse than feeling helpless to comfort your kids when they need it the most.

After a fairly sleepless night, Andy was slightly improved in the morning, so we forged on, it's a four-hour drive from Denver up over Independence Pass to Aspen, and then on to resort I had booked for the week. Not more than an hour into the drive, I glanced in the mirror and my son looked like he was literally disintegrating from the outside in. His skin was starting to come off in sheets. He was miserable and we were baffled. His sister did her best to comfort him until we arrived at our destination.

Eventually we checked in, got our room, unpacked and took in the amazing views. But, because he wasn't getting any better by the next morning the decision was made, that everyone else would fly back to Chicago to get Andy checked out. So, it was off to the Pitkin County Airport, the three of them boarded a plane bound for Chicago and I waved from the parking lot as my family headed home.

Okay, now what?

The best course of action was to stick with the plan at hand. For the next three days, I drove from the resort early in the morning to the Aspen Music Tent and returned late in the evening after attending lectures headed by speakers: Dennis Weaver, Linda Ellerbee, Chief Oren Lyons, Barbara Pyle, and Ed Begley Jr. A sea of incredible people from around the world attended in part because of the message of Windstar and in larger part because of the energy and leadership of John Denver.

On the final night of the symposium, the Windstar Award was being given to Phil Lane Jr., the founder and chairman of the Four World's International Institute, an organization dedicated to "Unifying the Human Family through the Fourth Way." The stage was filled with thousands of stones that had been placed in a "nautilus" shape, an ever-expanding circle that spoke to the circle of life. One hundred members of The Kainai Nation (Blood Tribe) had traveled from Alberta, Canada and sat in a semi-circle on the stage, and after some heartfelt words, John Denver presented the award to Chief Phil Lane Jr., who was wearing a full ceremonial headdress for the honor.

Men seated on the stage began to pound on drums and it seemed as if the music tent became a living, breathing organism, pulsating with the energy of 2,000 people. I stood in the back row of the tent, watching all this happen and I had an overwhelming urge to go out to the truck and retrieve a piece of wood I had carved an eagle head on, prior to the trip out west. I'd put the thing in the back of the Ford with no particular thought of why. Furthermore, I have no idea why I even carved it in the first place. I got a "C" in woodshop back in high school and it wasn't something I even considered a hobby, but I had sat for quite a few afternoons on the back porch, carving away.

I grabbed the stick, turned around, and it was an incredible sight.

There I was, just about 8,000 feet up in the middle of the Rockies, the sky was filled with billons of stars, more than I had ever seen in my life. Looking at the tent from the parking lot, it was lit up like a beacon, illuminating the night sky. The drumming, singing, and light filling the mountains and echoing the vibration. I went back in, made my way down the aisle and right up to the stage, went over to Phil Lane Jr. and said, "I think this is for you."

He looked at me and said… *"Yes, I have been waiting for this."*

Wait…*what?*

How is it possible that a blue-collar Chicago guy carved a piece of wood found in a forest preserve 1,000 miles away, and gave a "staff" right on time, to a chief of the Ihanktonwan Dakota and Chickasaw Nations, whom I had never even heard of before?

He smiled and I remember just walking off the stage in a bit of daze, as the celebration continued.

Later that night, I was driving back to the resort, filled with energy of the experience, feeling very light, open and a bit "transparent" for lack of a better term. When I drove up the entrance to the place, I noticed a set of tire tracks off to the left, heading up to a bit of a plateau, and then disappearing into the trees. I stopped the truck and sat there in the cool night air, as it seemed something was inviting me to follow those tracks.

Uh...*no*.

It had to be near midnight, its pitch black and it's not my truck, so, I declined the unspoken invitation and headed back to the resort because I was scheduled to be leaving the next day for the drive back to Chicago.

The news from home was good. I had checked in on Andy every day since they had left and was happy to hear that he was on the mend, but the docs were still baffled about his condition. So, after a great night's sleep I was up early the next morning, had the truck packed and ready to go. I thanked the people at the resort and assured them I would write a glowing review and started out of the access road towards the highway, but I didn't get far.

As I started the drive out of the resort, I glanced up at the side of the mountain. Those tire tracks. *Where did they lead to?*

I sat there, staring up at the steep incline and felt like a magnet was pulling me in that direction. I backed up, put the truck in four-wheel drive and climbed up the side of the ravine, hoping I wasn't tearing off the muffler or something. Following the little dirt road around a U-shaped bend, I made it to the top in short order and found myself overlooking the Roaring Fork Valley. I got out, walked to the edge of where I just drove up and glanced over.

Great, okay, nice view, big deal, I need to get going. As I turned to leave, I quickly realized I was standing in a cemetery.

There was no gate or sign, and I thought surely, they don't do burials by driving up the side of the mountain, do they? I figured that I must have come in on a back road of some sort. I took a deep breath of clear, mountain air and started back to the truck when I saw a child's toy next to a grave marker. "Michael Hill" was etched in the white stone; he was born just shortly after my son in 1991 and had only lived a few months.

I was suddenly overcome with emotion, sat down next to the little headstone and simply cried my eyes out, without really even knowing why. Finally, after a few minutes, I composed myself and said out loud, "If you have to spend eternity somewhere, this would be the place."

"I like it here" whispered a quiet but very clear voice in my head.

*"What the fu…*what?"

Nothing more. I sat for a few minutes, paid my respects and got ready to leave. The same voice stopped me.

"Please tell my mom and dad that I am okay. Please tell them that this is how it was supposed to be. Please tell them I love them. They are very sad."

I don't like it when a voice, or a message floats in, because initially I don't understand why it's happening.

So, I sat back down for about half an hour, and just listened to the wind and the faint words that rolled in and out of my head.

While the messages were clear; the would-be messenger was a wreck.

I had the overwhelming feeling that I was strongly being "moved" to find the little boy's parents and tell them that he was okay, that they should not feel guilty because they didn't do anything wrong and…as if that wasn't enough…tell them that within a year, they would have another child.

Shit, how would I? How could I?

When I finally felt "complete" at the grave, I drove back down to the hotel, asked if I could still get back in my room, they agreed and gave me a key. I sat on the bed, opened the phone book and found the numbers for two local funeral homes in the area. No response at the first one, but the second one answered. My voice stammered as I asked if they had done a funeral for a little boy named Hill, just over a year prior, in 1991.

The funeral director said that he had in fact taken care of that burial and *wanted to know why I wanted to know.*

Yeah…so did I. I asked him to just please contact the parents, give them my room number, and that I was heading out of town within the hour, because I needed to talk with them. I have no doubt he thought I was some sort of whack-job, and when I hung up the phone, it's possible he was right.

I had already pushed the boundary of my belief system past the point of no return, and while I felt a little relieved, part of me hoped that the funeral guy wrote me off and would never contact the parents. I wouldn't blame him. I just wanted to start heading home, but I waited about twenty minutes and decided that was that. I had done my duty to the best of my ability, or at least attempted to honor the experience as best I could, without really understanding any of it.

I bagged it, tagged it, and headed out of the room, down the stairs to the foyer of the resort, found a chair to catch my breath, and that's when I saw a familiar face.

A year earlier, I had done a few months of consulting work in Aspen, a chance I took thinking it would further and solidify my career as a personal trainer and while it was difficult to be away from my family, waking up in the Rocky Mountains took the edge off a little bit. One of the people that I met during that time was Tina and there she was walking right in front of me at the resort.

I called out to her, she came over with a big smile and as we reconnected, I made the best small talk I could, about the impact of the symposium and what had been going on with Andy. All of a sudden, I felt a very strong urge to share with her what had taken place, up on that ridge, just beyond the tree line. I needed to get it out of my head and off my chest.

She listened intently, but very quietly with almost no expression, When I finished, she got a bit teary eyed and said, "John, I know that family."

It was like a damn breaking...the energy simply rolled out of me at that point, overwhelming me even more than I already was. My hands trembled, sweat poured down my back.

I asked her if she would consider sharing what had happened with the boy's family and she agreed. Tina gave me her phone number, I thanked her and that was that.

I had run my part of the race and the baton was passed to someone that could take it to the finish line.

On the drive back to Chicago every time I stopped for gas, I found a payphone and called Tina, but it wasn't until a few days after I got home, that she called me back. She had shared the experience and messages, the parents cried and laughed at the same time. She said it had brought them a great measure of relief from the unmitigated pain they had been living in.

So, what are the odds I would take a three month foray into Aspen, then a year later drive back to the mountains for an event, my son gets some sort of affliction that has my family leaving me in the resort alone, so I could give a stick that I carved months earlier, not knowing why, to Phil Lane Jr., who is expecting it? Furthermore, I am sure that part of me going it solo was so I would drive up to that spot overlooking the valley to get the download that was needed, to pass it along to Tina, who then delivered it to those grieving parents.

After that last phone call from Tina, I never heard from her again, so I don't know what became of those young parents who "lost" their infant boy and how they managed to live with that pain and what joy they might have been able to find in their lives.

But, as I finish this chapter, I am once again fairly emotional about an experience that took place nearly 27 years ago. Events that impact our lives, both good and bad, positive and negative, do not have a time limit on them.

For me the lesson out of this experience is the opportunity for spiritual growth that exists when we have a deep loss, which often gets lost in the emotion of grief. The reminder that tomorrow is promised to no one (and neither is today) and the moment at hand is really all we have. It may not seem like it, but grief is a wakeup call of the highest order. The never-ending cycle of life that takes us over the same roads again and again to learn from different experiences, at varying levels of consciousness, is to make sure we stay awake, and that we need to pay attention to what is being offered, even if it's disguised as unbearable pain.

We become more aware of the gift of life, every time we are confronted by death, which is a concept that the ego has a hard time with, until it happens to someone close to us. Then, we are laid bare, and at our most vulnerable, but also more alive as grief reveals our hearts when they are most needed-and all that is unnecessary is washed away.

Every now and then, I think of that time in the mountains, how the "connect-a-dots" all lined up, and the importance of following the tracks, wherever they might lead.

-5-

SACRED GROUND

Disclaimer: There is zero chance I can clearly and accurately convey all that I was witness to in the years my family and I lived in Rapid River, in the Upper Peninsula of Michigan, because it's truly volumes of experiences, both great and small.

However, I would be remiss if I didn't at least attempt to share some of the sacred moments, memories, and messages along with other shit I can't explain to this day. If you would have told me that part of my journey would include sitting in front of a sacred fire for countless hours in a Native American lodge (often in sub-zero temps) that at times seemed to expand and contract because of the energy of people from all over the world, who openly shared their lives and experiences, I would have said...*NO WAY.*

But as it turns out it was... IT WAS THE WAY.

****

In early fall of 1994, my pal Dan was leading a teambuilding event for a hockey team in lower Michigan and I tagged along. We left Chicago early in the morning, got there ahead of schedule, and Dan facilitated the exercises, based on experiential education which are designed to get everyone working in the same direction, and towards a common goal (no pun intended). On the way back, we took a detour to a "gathering." We pulled up, and walked into this large dome shaped tent, filled with about forty people. There happened to be two chairs available to the immediate right of the entry way, so Dan sat in the chair nearest the door, and I sat next to him.

Then, a ruddy faced man with a very distinct voice and long flowing hair says, "Now we can begin." He began to speak in a Native American language, none of which I understood. Dan nudged me and said, "That's Earl. Pay attention to what he says."

For quite some time, this man talked softly but firmly about many things of a spiritual nature. Finally, when he finished, the eagle feather he had been holding was passed around, and for what seemed like an eternity, people spoke about their lives, hopes, dreams, fears, and faith.

I'd never experienced anything like this communal sharing, and I realized at some point, I was going to have to speak, out of respect for the place, if nothing else.

Then came my turn to stand up in front of all these strangers. I accepted the feather from the woman on my right and not knowing what to say, and feeling like there was no way I could possibly say anything as profound as what I had heard already, I just muttered, "I am glad to be here today."

That's all I could think of in the moment.

I passed the feather to Dan, who spoke a bit about his journey and the importance of recognizing the path, especially when it's the most difficult to see it. The ceremony finished up, and suddenly people began giving each other gifts. Food, blankets, incredible jewelry, drums, feathers and books. I felt very much unprepared and out of place, as I had nothing tangible to share. I kept to myself, off near the door, when Earl made his way towards me.

"You know, don't you?" he said.

"*Know what?*" I replied. As the years have gone by, I've pondered the question that Earl asked me many times, still not sure I have an answer.

At one point during our trip home we came across a red fox that had been hit in the middle of the road, and we both wondered how this cunning animal didn't see the danger that would end its life. Perhaps it had been so focused on something in the distance, it wasn't aware of what was coming towards it, that which was imminent.

Just a few months later, I was invited over to my friend Alison's house. On Halloween she was the photographer at the "Haunted Forest" where I had volunteered my time to be the final act as the Wolfman. Once people made it through all the other monsters, ghouls and creepy things, they could get their picture taken with me, fangs, claws, and all. She was having some of her Native American friends over and after that trip with Dan, I was intrigued. As it turned out, the man that many of her friends had come to visit with, was none other than Earl, the same guy I met in that ceremony back in Michigan.

Hmm.

I wasn't in the house more than five minutes, and then, a most incredible occurrence.

While Alison and her friends were gathered in the kitchen, I excused myself to the living room, plopped down on the couch and promptly fell asleep. This tends to happen to my body, when my ego, or mind needs to be moved aside for some sort of download to take place.

I had a powerful dream.

In it, I was standing on the edge of the forest, look-ing at a clearing, with a small fire burning in the middle. Suddenly, the trees parted to my left, and a huge bear came out of the woods, started circling the fire and finally stopped directly in front of me. Then, the bear began to dig at the ground, swaying back and forth on its front paws, left to right, right to left. It was not making any sound, but it just kept going back and forth, faster and faster, until I was able to finally snap myself awake, from the sheer ener-gy of the "vision."

I woke up, my heart racing a bit, but I was no longer alone in the living room, there was Earl, sitting in a corner chair, watching me.

"What did you dream?"

I sat up, looked around, and while there was noise coming from the kitchen, the room we were in felt like a vacuum. I told Earl what I had seen in that dream, and then he began to ask me a slew of questions.

"Do you know the direction you were standing in?"

"The east."

"What direction did the bear come from?"

"The west."

"How many times did it walk around the circle?"

"Six, or maybe seven. Yea, seven."

"What color was it?"

"White. But not a polar bear, just a white bear."

Earl just sat in the chair, listening and then nodding after each answer.

Finally, after a time, he got up and asked someone to get his "bundle" from the car. They did, and then he proceeded to take out this incredible array of sacred objects: pipes, pouches, pictures, sweetgrass, necklaces, bones, and a bunch of other things that he'd been carrying around for years.

"*Aanii* (Greetings) *Boozho* (Hello) *Ndishnikaaz* (I am) *Ogima Anaquot*" (Chief Cloud).

He then put all of his most sacred things on the blanket he had rolled out in front of the unlit fireplace and proceeded to pick up each and every object, speak to it in his language, and then put it down. By this time, everyone who was at the house was crowded in the living room, watching.

It took a very long time.

When he finished, he took out some cedar and put it in what looked like a clam shell, and lit it up, creating a thick smoke and then he used an eagle feather to carefully fan over everything on the blanket. The smell was pungent and intoxicating, ancient, and on purpose.

Then, he smudged all of us with the smoke, and finally, himself. As the energy in the room began to return to normal, I asked him what this was all about.

"That was a dream that I was waiting for and it came through you. The bear was telling me that I needed to become reconnected to my medicine, or I should put all of it in the fire and start over. This was a test from *Gitchie Manito* (Great Mystery) that came through my brother *Wabiska Mukwa* (White Bear) from the *Ninggabeuhnoong* (West direction). So, for that I say, "*Miigwetch*" (Thank you).

I then watched him carefully return every single item back into his bundle, taking time to thank each feather, bone, stone and braid of sweetgrass, showing deep appreciation for the gifts he had been given.

When Earl finished, he gave me a quick smile and nod, as I sat on the couch, letting the rest of the energy drain off me.

Earl

While that dream didn't mean anything to me, it *meant everything to him*. To watch this man, offer up his most sacred objects, and be willing to let them go in order to begin his spiritual quest all over again, is a memory that has stayed with me these many years.

****

Nine months later, in fall of 1995, I was heading over to Northeastern Illinois University to hear a talk about sports management (or so I thought). My football days were long behind me, and even though I had finally earned my college degree in communications, my time spent around pro athletes had me thinking about taking a course or two, in the direction of becoming an agent. When I got to the room where the talk was supposed to be happening none of the people looked anything like sporting types, dressed more like the Lewis & Clark expedition, or frontier folks from a time past, a few of them with long hair and beaded, fringe jackets. There were about twenty people in attendance, the woman at the front was getting ready to start her presentation, so I got up, checked the room number on the flyer, which was correct, but I got the distinct impression that sports of any kind, was not on the agenda.

So, I sat back down and thought I'd stay a few minutes. An hour later, I was still there, fascinated at what was being offered by noted historian and author, the late Dr. Helen Hornbeck Tanner. She was sharing her knowledge of the Ojibwe and Odawa people, whom she had spent much time with around her home in the Great Lakes area. I had never paid much attention to anything in that direction at all, but over the years, more and more "spiritual people" had been showing up in my life, and the way she spoke about her experiences, and stories of the Native America culture and way of life, had me hooked in the cheek.

When the program was over, Dan, (who I didn't see when I walked in) flagged me down and said he wanted to introduce me to some very special people. First up was Bruce, a stout man with a broad face, intense eyes, and flowing white hair down to his shoulders. Then his cousin Duane stepped in close and instead of shaking my hand, he hugged me and laughed, eyes twinkling, long hair like Bruce's, but much darker.

But what struck me the most, were the big buttons featuring children's photographs on them that were pinned on Duane's coat. His children I guessed. In conversation, I learned that they were indeed his kids, Aaron and Liz, it was something the schools did in the Upper Peninsula of Michigan, where they lived. We talked for a bit, exchanged phone numbers and promised to stay in touch.

After that chance meeting, dozens of phone calls between the Northwest side of Chicago and the UP occurred and somehow in conversation with Bruce's wife, Pat, she asked if I would consider presenting the commencement address at her son Tom's graduation.

Sure...uh, *where is the Upper Peninsula?*

****

I took Pat up on her offer and on Memorial Day weekend of 1996, I hauled my family north, towards the UP. Until that trip, Green Bay, Wisconsin was as far as I had been on family vacations as a boy. Breaking the invisible boundary where US 43 connects with 41 North, was a rite of passage, a new and unexplored land lie ahead, especially when the driving the two-lane artery of M35, next to the furthest reaches of Lake Michigan, a route that back then was foreign, but would become familiar over the years, a connecting road between Wisconsin and Upper Michigan.

On that first trip, I was introduced to The Lodge, a massive, turtle shell like structure, made by many human hands, tied together in a traditional way, a crisscrossing of sturdy branches and poles, creating a portal of sorts, twenty or more feet high in the center. It was a much larger structure than where I had met Earl. The levels of energy not only went up towards the sky, but also down into the Earth, and was located near the tree line behind the Hillcrest Motel, owned by Bruce and Pat. I had no way of knowing it then but my family would eventually live at the motel for a year, which is a book in and of itself.

As the elder and firekeeper, Bruce usually struck the fires (lit in celebration or the changing of the seasons, or by request) a tradition he learned from his teacher, the late Dale Thomas *"Nowaten"* (He Who Listens). He'd pull out his bag that was filled with all manner of stones, pipes, and *sktagin*, (fungus from the White Birch) and slowly load up the wood needed in the center of the four main lodge poles. He'd then take a piece of newspaper, stuffing the sacred tobacco plant in the middle, and with a flint, make strike after strike, until a spark caught a piece of sktagin. Then slowly walking around in a circle in The Lodge, he'd fan the smoking embers with an eagle feather, until a larger flame appeared, then he placed the burning paper mix into fire pit, to which larger pieces of wood were added.

Every strike of that flint, every step of his walk around the sacred circle, every wave of that feather, had a meaning to him, and became the foundation for the way that particular fire would go. After the flames were dancing on their own, Bruce would introduce himself to those in the circle and all his relations in the world…in his native language…

"*Boozhoo* (Hello) *Aanii* (Welcome) *Ndishnikaaz* (I am) *Muk-Ta-The'* (Gray Striped Wolf) *Skush* (Blue) of The Wolf Clan."

Bruce

He would then remind us that this was sacred ground that we were sitting, standing, walking, and talking on. That it was a place of non-judgment and acceptance. Bruce would pass the feather to someone in the circle, who would then take as much time as needed. I'd never been in a space where someone could get up and "share" whatever it might be in their heart or on their mind, and everyone in attendance (who kinda just showed up) sat and listened, for as long as the person wanted to talk, sometimes for hours, in the darkest part of night, in the bitter cold of winter and the heat of late summer. A little different than how we worshipped back at the Irving Park Presbyterian Church. Every single time I entered the door of The Lodge from the east, I picked up a pinch of tobacco and placed it in the center between those four poles, fire or not, I was transported to a different energy, something far more pure than my ego, a light that seemed to push back on the darkness, and replace doubt...with faith.

The tobacco is used as an offering to the Creator, or a gift to someone and a sign of respect, asking for help, guidance, or protection. I carry a leather pouch with a small amount of tobacco in my left pants pocket every day.

It's the one thing that seems to ground and connect me back to that sacred place and people, no matter where I go.

****

Some of the most incredible acts of courage I've ever witnessed, took place in The Lodge. With its lofty center, and square opening in the center for the smoke to pour out, tokens, pouches, pictures, and remembrances from people from literally every background, and from the far corners of the globe, it was a formidable haven for those who were lost but yet somehow found their way to this sacred place. They had been abused, raped, injured, given up hope, lost their way, criminals, clergy, teachers, shamans, parents who lost children, children who lost parents. Strangers, scientists, Tibetan holy men, homeless wanderers, NFL legends, pro bodybuilders, celebrated authors, television stars, congressmen, to name just a few, all shared their heartbreak and triumphs, scars and stars, tears, and fears.

While there are countless memories and moments from those years, I recall the time when two German guys just "happened" to drop in...

The parking lot of the motel was getting a new coat of black top. Pat's son Tom, Duane, and I had moved the parking bumpers out of the way so the work could be done, and later in the day once the lot was ready to go, we were lifting the concrete barriers up and putting them back. No sooner had we finished, a car goes speeding by the motel, heading east, which caught our attention. Just minutes later, the same car comes pulling into the driveway with two men in it.

It took about five seconds to figure out they were not locals, matter of fact they weren't even Americans. In a heavy accent, the younger man asked about getting a room. I took him in to meet Pat, and the older man sat in the car, quietly nodding his head. Bruce was not home, and shortly the young man came out, spoke German to the other fellow, and while it had been years since *Ich sprach Deutsch in die Oberschule* (high school), I picked up that they were father and son. While Duane and I sat out front of the place, the men got their room and then came back out a few minutes later.

Duane nudged me and said, "Maybe you should take them out to The Lodge."

"Why don't *you* take them out there. You're the Native American guy here, not me."

"Because you are part German and you understood some of what they were saying, didn't ya?"

Ich haase es, wenn er Recht hat. Translation: I hate it when he's right.

So, I introduced myself, the young man spoke fairly good English, and then conveyed to his father, that I wanted to show them a place in the rear of the property.

The man nodded, and we started walking, and I learned they had decided to go "traveling in America," flying in from Stuttgart, where the father worked as an engineer for Mercedes-Benz for many years and had recently retired. They grabbed a rental car in Milwaukee that morning, looked at a map, and headed north until they found themselves in Rapid River.

"You guys were driving pretty fast you know. What made you turn around?"

"Yes, we drive fast, but when we drove past the motel, my father insisted we go back and stay for the night. He reads energy like that."

"He reads what?"

By the time the son and I got to the door of The Lodge, the father had walked in and was sitting in the big chair in the south that Bruce usually sat in. It was odd to see someone else there, most times when the "turtle shell" was filling with people, no one ever sat in that chair, even if they had never been there before.

But there he sat.

The son and I made small talk, sitting in the first two chairs to the left of the entrance, I did my best to explain what took place here, the ceremony and songs, the fires and people, who also seem to just "show up" as needed.

The father closed his eyes for a long time, then started speaking German, only bits and pieces of which I understood, and the son began to translate for me.

"He's praying now. Reading the energy of this place."

"I thought he worked as an engineer."

"He did, and his gift was to be able to create something from nothing by accessing the energy of ideas."

Alrighty then.

Eventually, the man got up from the chair and started walking around the circle, first in the clockwise direction, for about five minutes, then suddenly, started going backwards, counterclockwise until he got to a mid-point in the northwest direction.

He stopped, put out his hands in front of him, palms just inches from the ground and spoke in German to his son, *"Er sagt, dass das dasselbe Energiefeld ist, das er im Apostolischen Palast fühlte, als wir dort zwei Wochen her waren. Es gibt eine Richtungsverbindung zwischen dem Punkt, den er auf und die Sixtinische Kapelle stehend auf."*

"He says this is the same energy field he felt in the Apostolic Palace when we were there two weeks ago. There is a direct connection between the spot he is standing on and the Sistine Chapel." His matter of fact tone left no room for anything from me but, "Uh...*okay.*"

The man clasped his hands together, recited what sounded like The Lord's Prayer, walked back around the circle, bowing in each direction, and walked out of The Lodge.

The son thanked me, shook my hand, and they went back to their room and left at some point during the night, continuing their journey. We never saw them again.

****

I've struggled a bit with this chapter, because while I can describe the physical structure of The Lodge, it's the *metaphysical* that cannot be easily communicated. It was remarkable to watch people stand up at the fire, in front of total strangers, and totally spill out their spiritual guts. I lost count of the times I was witness to those who felt that their religion fell short of expectation or comfort and just wanted to be accepted for who they were, and not judged by who others for who they were not. Years of trying to live up to strict religious guidelines, burdened by guilt, and wracked with pain for having lost faith in the God they believed was sitting on a throne, judging them.

Through the non-judgment of all of us who sat listening, no matter how many hours it took to vomit up all that had held them back from becoming a viable member of the human family, they began to rise from the ashes.

And, the biggest reason for universal acceptance in the sacred circle?

Every time someone got up and began to speak, while their experiences were different, the lessons, teachings, and words could have been our own and most of the time, they were. It didn't take long for someone to see themselves in another, and the truth is that we are all up against it in some way, shape, or form.

We just pretend that we are not, hiding behind the firewall of "I'm fine."

But as Earl has said, "We are the ones we've been waiting for." It takes a measured amount of faith to understand and accept those words, and serious courage to live them.

Perhaps if we knew how difficult our path would be, we would hesitate, hold back, and not make the journey. As Bruce would often say, "It's easy in The Lodge, to stand before the fire and speak your truth. Much harder to do it out in the world, but that is truly where it matters most."

The forgiveness (for ourselves and each other) that was generated in The Lodge at every single fire, created a healing balm of sorts, a palpable energy that became an anointing for all who were there, whether we sang the songs or not, spoke our truth or sat quiet, fell asleep, or danced in the circle.

****

Pat

In 2015, the universal connect-a-dots lined up, and a new owner took over The Hillcrest Motel, who is very much aware of its sacred past. Bruce, Pat, Duane, and the rest of us have moved into new chapters of our lives but remain connected to (and through) The Lodge, the place where all people were welcomed home.

As I sit here recalling all of this, (and much more) it's clear to me once again that a very powerful ripple effect took place in those twenty years up north, and while we no longer sit together in the circle as we once did, the concentric rings from that time continue on, as each of us that stood on sacred ground, carries the teachings, lessons, and energy of that time with us.

"This is the only road there is, when you realize you are no longer satisfied with the way things are. You become a seeker of the truth. Not somebody else's, but your own."

Dale Thomas *"Nowaten"* (He Who Listens)

6

TREE OF HOPE

I have an odd habit of working from the top down when it comes to writing. Before I even typed a single word for this book, I needed to know what the title, subtitle, and basic theme was going to be. So, starting at the top allows me to work my way down the list of things I'd like to include, which helps me create a "ladder of words" as it were, that I can descend, which is the usual drill for me.

Normally, I layout the chapters by proceeding in an orderly straight line fashion by first creating the Author's Preface, then writing all the chapter drafts and then, cleaning them up by adding or subtracting text, enhancing or toning down, making adjustments along the way before laying out the book, then I can start to read it through from stem to stern, as you, the reader, eventually will.

However, this book has been a little different.

While these chapters are not in chronological order on paper, in my mind they are connected in some way, shape, or form even though it might not appear that way and often those threads only become clear to me when I am writing. My initial draft of Chapter 6 was only one page with a couple of notes, and if my writing timeline held up, I should have been working on this chapter just after finishing "Sacred Ground", Chapter 5 and before "Sweet Surrender", Chapter 7.

That didn't happen.

I have skipped over this chapter, glancing at the blank space a dozen times, not exactly sure why I had to wait for this to be the very last chapter I actually wrote.

A few theories have crossed my mind.

First, that I won't be able to do justice to the experience and that any words needed to convey all that took place on The Walk would be inadequate. It was a dream that became the first domino, that would set everything else in motion, but it was only one of the many dominoes in a chain of events. *Second*, the people who walked with us, like the elderly lady who only had enough energy to walk down the length of her driveway, or the people who started out walking from The Lodge that September morning, like the late, great Dan Gobert (who made it two miles, dressed in his Sunday best, as we headed towards Escanaba,) along with everyone that fed us, housed us, interviewed us, tended the fires, and watched this all unfold (especially my family) all have their own unique remembrances, versions, and chapters, interwoven with mine. Untangling all that is a daunting mental and literary task. *Third,* the roots of this journey go back nearly 24 years, and while some of it shows up as a clearly framed image, much of what took place has been lost to the dusty corners of my mind. *Fourth,* I've written about this experience before, back in 2006 and 2010, so why would I include it again in this book?

Because while it's true that I physically finished The Walk over two decades ago, on a metaphysical level, it never really ended. Like many life altering events, on a spiritual, emotional, and even psychological level, it continues to teach, instruct, remind, and even heal me at times, and for those reasons The Walk needed to be included in this work.

****

Back in the 4th century BC, the ancient Chinese philosopher and writer Lao-Tzu said, *"The journey of a thousand miles begins with the first step."* Well, I don't know if Mr. Tzu ever actually walked a thousand miles, but I have, and at the risk of challenging one of the great teachers of wisdom in human history, I can tell you that the first step isn't on foot, but rather in the mind.

Actually, for me, it was in a series of dreams.

The first dream I had was in late December 1995, not long before Christmas. No idea what prompted it, nor does that matter. In the dream I was walking through fire, walls of flame, towering infernos, and smoldering piles of ash. The fire seemed to form a maze of sorts, which I made my way through for a very long time. I kept walking this seeming endless path of fire, but to my amazement I was not harmed in any way, I didn't even feel the heat. Eventually, I came upon a corner where there was this figure that I knew was "The Creator." It was sitting on a large rock and the intensity of the fire that spewed from the figure was white-hot, a constant flow of what appeared to be lava poured down to the ground and was apparently the source of all the fire I had walked through.

"The Creator" looked like a large human, with discernable features, except no eyes. While odd looking, I had no fear about this entity that held my attention.

I felt like I was in the presence of the greatest energy source imaginable, as if the entire universe was powered from this one rock and the entity that sat on it.

"What is your question?" the entity asked me.

"Why don't you have any eyes?" I asked.

Without hesitation, came the reply, "Because I don't need them to see the truth *and neither do you.*"

Then I woke up.

Just writing these words, so many years later, I can clearly recall the dream as if it happened moments ago.

What followed that initial "fire walk dream" was a most remarkable, sacred, gathering of moments, memories, and messages and shit I still cannot explain.

****

The second dream was series of recurring dreams, my subconscious created in order to get past the firewall of my sensibilities, to show me the journey that became The Walk. It was just a snapshot really, a short-framed image that burned into my mind over and over again, placed against a background of change in my waking life.

In this dream I stood on a curved piece of road, a stick or staff of some sort in my right hand. My head was looking towards what I knew to be the west, as the sun was setting across a pond or small lake and it was a warm day. A formidable beard framed my face, a sturdy backpack hung off my shoulders, the dark edge of a forest was to the east and only the jutting branches of pine trees were clear to me. I viewed myself from behind and above. I was motionless, frozen on that spot, gazing in the distance, as if listening or looking for something.

Then I would wake up.

This dream was always taking place moments before I opened my eyes, and I would shake myself a bit, as you do when you feel you are somehow coming back into your body.

This happened on a steady schedule, just about every other day, for months, and always the same images at the same time, just before waking. On some level it was maddening, as I had zero idea what it meant, and on the other hand, it seemed to coincide with the changes going on at the time. Looking back on it all these years later, it seems like a lifeline of sorts, something that I could focus on in my mind, when everything else seemed so scattered.

At some point during this "dream thing" another "phenomenon" began to manifest, the physical sensation that felt like someone was slowly dragging their finger over my forehead, from my right ear to my left, almost as if opening up a zipper or something. It was the strangest feeling, at times light as a feather, other times a more insistent and direct pressure.

It was then that I began to research a bit about the concept of "the third eye" located in the middle forehead, between the eyebrows; the exact spot I felt that "tingling." The third eye is a state of enlightenment or the bringing forth of mental imagery having deeply emotional, spiritual or psychological importance.

That's great on paper, but in real life, all of it seemed to be an indicator that I was losing my shit, which at the time would understandable because of everything I was going through.

A business deal I thought would be the "golden ticket" fell apart, and no matter who I called, or what I tried, nothing seemed to work. Slowly the walls began to close in and after much angst, I reached out to new friends, Bruce and Pat. Over many conversations since our first trip north, the connection had grown stronger and at one point I was on the phone with Bruce, telling him that I couldn't find my way "out" of the chaos my family was going through, that somehow seemed to be out of my control to avoid.

Finally, he said, "Why don't you come up here to live?"

I responded with, "What the hell would I do up there? Bruce replied, "What the hell are you gonna do that hasn't already been done down there?

For better or for worse turmoil seems to be the catalyst for change and I think to some extent we each get to determine the "better" or "worse" depending on our consciousness and/or perspective. What often seems like an ending, is a beginning in disguise, and vice-versa. There was nothing in my conscious mind that would have led me to think that it was a great idea to lose our home, and move into a little motel in Upper Michigan. We left Chicago, with a mixture of being "called" without knowing why, and a visceral fear of what the future held for us. At least, that's how I felt at the time.

I was 37, had served my country, earned a college degree, worked my ass off at various jobs, thought I had followed the "rules" and now I was apparently a failure on some level, as my family and I would be living in a kitchenette, surrounded by people we had only met within the past year. There was no way to know how this was all going to roll out.

With the four of us stuffed into two rooms, I couldn't help but think that I had lost whatever marbles I might have left. I was not alone as other voices chimed in, including my family and a few friends who challenged the decision to move (and rightfully so). Then, about three weeks after the move, part of the puzzle re-appeared…that dream of walking rose up from my subconscious once again.

But this time, I had someone who might be able to help me understand it.

I went directly to Bruce, told him what had happened, he then took me out back to The Lodge and said I was being given a choice, "You can go back the way you came, or find out what The Mystery is calling you to do."

We had a long talk, and I chose the second option, further putting myself so far out of my comfort zone, that I couldn't believe it. I *knew* that I had to walk from Rapid River to Chicago *and back*. I had no idea that two men would join me. Duane had been "waiting for me" and Joe, felt "called" to the journey.

In my second book *Every Moment Matters* there is a chapter entitled, "The Last Hundred Miles" that fills in many of the other puzzle pieces, so I will not use this space to recount those moments. However, there are a couple of sacred moments, messages, and memories, I haven't shared before.

Like the night we spent in Whitewater, Wisconsin.

Duane, Joe, and I had chain of support laid out for us, people that knew we were walking and assisted us in various ways. This particular time, it was getting darker and colder, as fall was fast approaching. Word of our trek had gotten to the owners of a Victorian style bed and breakfast, who offered to put us up for the night. Duane and I shared a room with two beds, Joe got his own room downstairs. The three of us sat for a time in the main kitch en, talking about the day and before long it was time to get some rest, as we would be heading further south, at first light.

At some point in the middle of the night, I heard someone talking, but it was unintelligible. It would come and go, I figured it must have been the owners downstairs playing cards or something. I tried my best to ignore it, until finally I realized it was Duane, who was mumbling in his sleep. I turned on the small lamp next to the bed, and as my eyes adjusted, I could have sworn there was a person standing in the corner of the room, and there on the bed across from me, was Duane twitching around like he was being electrocuted or something.

I first thought I must be dreaming, but then of course, I was awake, right?

Duane's mumbling got louder and louder, and he was starting to move up and down like on a roller coaster-all I could think of was *"The Exorcist"* and I wasn't having any of that shit.

I got up, turned all the lights on and tried to wake him up, which took some doing. I told him what happened, and while he was bleary eyed, he said, "I dreamed that the 'old ones' were working on me. I watched the whole thing from the corner of the room."

You gotta be shitting me. Was that Duane's "ethereal" body I saw when I turned on the light? What "old ones" was he talking about?

He said, "I'll be healed up in the morning. Turn out the light and let's get back to sleep."

Uh…*hell no.*

We (or should I say he) slept with the lights on the rest of the night.

Joe had slept soundly, with no apparent "visitors."

****

While stretches of the journey were boring, bland, and repetitive, there were times we felt "called" to a certain location or spot, and one of those times was on the shores of Lake Winnebago, six miles south of Oshkosh, Wisconsin.

Joe had been unable to walk for a couple of days, his youth and vigor (he was twenty-one) had put blisters on top of blisters, so he rode in the support van during this part of the trip. As Duane and I hoofed it down Route 45 through Black Wolf, Wisconsin, we saw a sign for the Jesuit Retreat House and immediately made a left turn to the access road, heading east. After a short trek, we found ourselves on the grounds of the retreat, the sparkling blue lake spread out before us like a mirror. All of a sudden Duane says, "Look, there's a lodge."

Nestled on a bank overlooking the water, stood a building, round in design with slotted windows, and above the arched doorway, the words, "Shrine of The Sacred Heart."

Huh.

We made our way to the little structure, went inside and found ourselves in a most sacred place. A narrow pathway encircled the perimeter of the shrine with chairs set up, not unlike The Lodge in Rapid River, where we had started the journey from weeks before. From every vantage point you could sit and look to the center of the building and gaze upon an alabaster looking statue of Jesus, with a small child on his lap. Sunlight streamed in from above and illuminated the space.

We sat for about fifteen minutes in silence, letting the energy of the location soak into our bones, restoring our spirits, and I think I even nodded off for a bit. Then we got up, made our way out to the main retreat area and began to walk back towards to van, when Duane says, "We need to go spend a few minutes with that tree," as he pointed back toward the lake front.

As we got closer, the tree looked like it had been struck by lightning at one point, and nearly split in two, a deep gash running up and down its trunk.

But it was still alive.

And, then a thunderbolt of realization came forth, that mangled, but still standing tree, was a reflection of me in so many ways.

On some level that is what The Walk was really all about. I was being "split in two." No longer able to just be who I had been, but another part of me was being revealed, a part of me that I didn't even know existed. I was answering the call, without even knowing why the spiritual phone was ringing. I was literally "walking by faith and not by sight." Words that look great in print, but are far more difficult to actually accomplish, for the most part, in real life.

As we stood there, a man walked up to us, introduced himself as one of the Jesuits and said, "I see you have been drawn to the 'Tree of Hope' as so many are. That tree is very special and at one time it was probably the

largest tree on the grounds. During a summer thunder-
storm, a lightning strike reduced its size to 25 feet or so.

At first, it was thought that it was time for the tree to go,
but it was not cut down; and then, someone realized that it
was growing a new set of leaves. To this day the very top
of the tree sprouts new leaves during every growing season. The tree has become something of a spiritual icon at

the retreat house. Many people find this tree a manifestation of God's enduring presence in their damaged and suffering lives."

I was overcome with emotion. Everything he said pertained to me in that moment.

Duane, as usual, just nodded his head.

The man smiled and said, "The Great Mystery always leads us to where we need to be, to learn what we need to learn, in order to become who, we really are."

I had heard nearly those same words from Bruce on the day I made the choice to walk, to find out what was waiting for me on the road, a reconnection to those parts of myself that had been washed away by the erosion of life.

****

As I traveled step by step, layers of my old self peeled off with every passing mile. After finally reaching Chicago, we took a short break, reconnecting with our families who met us there. Then Duane headed home, a couple days later, Joe took a Greyhound bus back, and I walked the return trip north *alone*. Eventually, I found myself just outside of Oconomowoc, Wisconsin, standing in the very scene I had been shown repeatedly in my recurring dream, a bearded seeker, fully laden pack, a long stick for support on a curved chunk of road, with the sun setting on my left.

How was that possible? How could I have been shown a "preview" of sorts, months before that moment? What was I supposed to do?

It was on that spot where the veil of reality became thin enough for me to finally get my divine assignment.

I clearly heard a voice, in bell-like tone… "*John, go on the radio.*"

It would take nearly a year from that "intervention" for me to find my way to talk radio and use that platform as a way to find the obvious truths buried in the absurdity of the chaos of life, and commit to make sense out of the senseless. While my calling became a twenty + year career, within the very core of all I do there is a deep responsibility that I feel to use the time I have been given, to honor that which has been asked of me.

As I sit here finishing up this chapter, the image in that dream of me on the side of the road, backpack, beard, stick in hand, sun setting on my left, is never far away from me, and has become my "true north" or internal compass.

The three of us were called to the road for many reasons, and a season, autumn specifically, a time of great change.

Duane, Joe, and John

While I've faltered many times on the path, I have never wavered from "the calling," all made possible because I literally "followed a dream" and was finally able to listen to the "still, small voice within." Once again came the lesson to trust the process and the path especially when I don't understand it or cannot see it, which, for the record, is most of the time.

But then again, what is the point of faith if we knew what was around every bend in the road?

There's a guy whom I strongly identify with on many levels that put it this way:

"Faith is to believe what you do not yet see; the reward for this faith is to see what you believe."

- St. Augustine of Hippo

7

SWEET SURRENDER

The most challenging aspect of reflecting and reviewing these "experiences" and "encounters," especially years later, is that I am concerned about how to adequately put words into some semblance of order. How to accurately convey the incredible, if not downright sacredness of each "experience" and "encounter." What it feels like swimming in them, a river of energy of sorts, that comes from a source so pure, that I knew all was as it should be, even if the core meaning was hidden to me at the time.

When mapping out the chapters I wanted to include in this book, this particular chapter was taken on and off the list three times. Why? Much of this experience is very personal to me. I've shared a bit of it in print before, but there is some sort of back current moving parts around again in order for me to get a clearer view of my journey, if I pay attention. So, despite some hedging in my mind, all that follows needed to be included.

That and the fact, I am convinced beyond all reasonable doubt, that I wouldn't be doing any of the "work" that

I have been involved in for the past 26 years, without the late John Denver pushing me in this direction.

****

I grew up in Chicago, on the northwest side of the city, a fairly idyllic childhood right near a big playground where I spent most of my time. Our house was right down the alley from the Keeler Avenue on-ramp to the outbound Kennedy Expressway, and my bedroom was on the second floor, both windows facing the constant sound of traffic, that seemed to never end. It was softball in the summer, ice skating on the flooded, asphalt surface in the winter, football in the fall, and an ongoing, endless stream of activity at that neighborhood hub.

In 1974, I had my first paying job, as a "porter" at Dunkin' Donuts, two miles from home. Not sure how I got the gig, but I started out with cleaning floors and toilets on the early shift, punching in at 4 a.m. and out at 7 a.m. four mornings a week. I'd get up at 3 a.m. then walk two miles from home to the Double D, work for three hours, stuff down some donuts and then walk to high school, another mile down Milwaukee Avenue. After school was football practice, then walk back another mile home, eat dinner, do homework, and hit the rack. It was a "lather, rinse, repeat" cycle existence, but I recall those early morning walks on dark, empty, sidewalks past homes of my friends who I knew were still asleep, through the Six Corners shopping area that was a ghost town before sunrise, and finally to the brightly lit building, that served coffee and donuts to the regulars at the crack of dawn.

On my very first morning, I met Michelle.

She had a bright smile, wonderful energy, and was a "veteran" of the place, while I was a mere rookie. After I swabbed the floors and stacked 50 lb. bags of flour, 'Shell would shove a double chocolate donut my way. I rinsed it down with a Grape Nehi, and while I think I was supposed to have any food docked from my pay substantial pay, ($1.65 cents an hour) I don't think she ever kept a tab.

At some point, I worked my way up the food chain (pun intended) and was trained as a baker. This was a huge deal for me, and in short order, I was rolling out dough in front of the large viewing window, a peep show of sorts for customers waiting in line. I got pretty good at it, learned how to crack two eggs in one hand at the same time, got a dime an hour bump in pay, made all the required donuts, (and a few I invented myself) and started a small side business by taking the donuts that would be tossed after twelve hours with me to school, and selling them for .25 cents each, until the lunchroom lady caught me.

Later that summer, Michelle invited me over to her house just blocks from my home, to "hear this guy's voice." So, on a warm summer evening, 46 years ago, I sat out on the porch of the brick two flat and heard these lyrics...

"Lost and alone on some forgotten highway, traveled by many, remembered by few. Looking for something that I can believe in, looking for something that I'd like to do...with my life."

A bolt of truth came from the stereo speakers set in the window and embedded itself in my fifteen-year-old soul. The lyrics were from a song called *Sweet Surrender* and "the guy" was John Denver.

Within the space of that song something shifted in me that I couldn't quite pinpoint, a convergence of sorts, and a course was set that wouldn't show itself for a very long time, but the destination was assured.

Not too long after that, I began to listen to more of Denver's music and message, which hit higher positive notes, in direct opposition of the headlines at the time, as

Vietnam was winding down, the stain of Watergate, and the eventual resignation of Nixon.

At some point in all of this, my mom picked up on the music thing. One day I came home from school to find that she had transformed my bedroom into a cabin of sorts, that could have been nestled in the Rockies. She had added a huge wall mural of the mountains that I looked at every night before I went to sleep, an escape route from the sound of highway traffic.

Fast forward to 1989.

I read in the newspaper that John was performing a one-man show called, "Higher Ground" focused on environmental and social responsibility, and I wanted to know more. As it turned out, he would be performing at The Chicago Theater, and I was able to get involved as part of the advance team to help market the event. At some point, I thought it was a good idea to call Bill Kurtis, (the well-known host of *Cold Case Files* and *American Justice*, and narrator on the *Anchorman* movies, along with a slew of other hits) but back then, he was the biggest name, along with Walter Jacobson, in Chicago news.

I left him a message on his desk phone at CBS, and sure enough the next evening as I was making my way down to the center of the third row, here comes Bill Kurtis from the other side of the aisle, we ended up sitting next to each other, taking in the performance and hanging out with John and a few VIP's after the show. That chance meeting with Bill, created a friendship that still endures thirty years later, the common denominator being our shared passion for the environment.

By November 1990, I was still chopping away at college and worked overnight security at the Ramada O'Hare, and because I was doing the third shift, sometimes I would watch *The Tonight Show with Jay Leno* before I went to work.

One night, I was sitting on the couch, tying my shoes when Leno said, *"You all know my next guest, mulitalented singer/songwriter, who will be performing at the Wang Center in Boston on December 3rd...John Denver!"*

All I heard in my head was, *"Go to the Wang Center on December 3rd."*

What? Go where? *Why?*

So, with no sense of logic, I called the airlines that night and bought a roundtrip ticket to Boston. On the morning of December 3rd, I flew out of Chicago carrying a large "prayer staff" that had been given to me by a fellow named "Whitefeather" a couple years earlier. Without having any idea of why I was going, I headed east, landed at Logan Airport, grabbed a taxi, and found my way to a small motel right next to the Atlantic Ocean. Once settled in my little room, I pulled out the phone book, and totally relying inner guidance, called the third hotel listed on the page, asked for Kris (John's road manager) and sure enough, he answered the phone. Kris said there was a fifteen-minute window to talk before the concert that evening, so got me a seat and said he would see me soon.

However, our time before the concert evaporated because of weather delays, and I ended up sitting in the Green Room eating cheeseburgers provided by Kris, surrounded by John's guitars being auto-tuned. The concert was great, John was in fine voice and after the show, I ended up standing in the dimly lit hallway downstairs. He finally came out; we shook hands and he asked me what was so important.

I replied, "I thought you'd know."

He cocked his head and said, "Did you bring me something?"

Actually, I had, without knowing it. There were a few letters in my coat pocket from kids who I had spoken to weeks earlier about the importance of environmental stewardship. I took them out, gave them to John and he read each one top to bottom.

It was at that point that he put his hand on my shoulder and asked me the question that has been reverberating for the past 30 years: *"Do you know that your voice matters?"*

I didn't.

He assured me that it did, and four years later, when John invited me to speak at Windstar in 1994, my mom claimed that it was the bedroom wall mural that put everything in place.

She might have been right about that.

Standing on that stage, speaking to a sea of humans crammed into the Aspen Music Tent became a serious pivot point in my life. I attribute much of my ongoing work in "the betterment of humanity" to JD's influence, friendship, and support. The thousands of radio shows, the books, and

TED talks that have followed over the years, all come from a simple question asked in the basement of a concert hall, one very snowy winter night.

Then, on Sunday, October 12, 1997, John died in a plane crash.

I heard about it on the car radio taking my kids to school early Monday morning. I had just started my radio show a month earlier, and JD was on the call sheet of guests for November. It was a gut punch and shot to the heart all at once.

Somehow, I muddled through the show, went home and headed over to see Bruce. I gave him tobacco and asked him to strike a fire for John. Bruce agreed, but said I would have to "tend" the fire over a four-day period. Once the fire was struck in The Lodge, I sat for a very long time thinking about John, the conversations we had over the years, and the impact one person can have on the world.

I had stepped away from the fire and was talking with Pat on the rear deck of the motel, when I suddenly saw my brother from another mother Duane, walking back towards the tree line, with a man by his side. When I asked Pat who it was, she said, "It's a guy named John, who is hitchhiking home and stopped here. Duane wants to show him The Lodge."

"What did you say his name was?"

"John, I think is what he said."

"Huh."

So, I followed them, and when I walked in, John had taken a seat in the southern direction, in a large chair, where Bruce usually sits. Duane was in the west and I took a seat directly across from this hitchhiker, in the north.

The man was wearing a loose-fitting green army coat, something you would get in a military surplus store. He had longish blond hair and spoke in an easy manner, but there was also sense of urgency in his voice. He spoke directly to Duane, and two things he said have stayed with me to this day. He wished he had spent more time with his children instead of "being on the road all the time" and that he loved being near water, and with the rain beating down on The Lodge roof like a drum, he kept tilting his head up, as if listening for something.

Then, he said that he really appreciated the time he had spent at the fire, but "it was time to get going home" and whistled softly, while the fire crackled.

Finally, the man looked across the burning wood and smoke at me, and for a fleeting moment or two, I swear the face I saw, wasn't the face of the man that walked in.

It was John Denver's.

He appeared to look to his left, then to the right, and then his face was gone, and there sat the hitchhiker. What the hell was that? What had I seen? Was it just my imagination or wishful thinking? Grief?

With that, I put a couple pieces of wood on the fire and left, more than a little shaken from the experience, and I told no one.

Later that evening, as the rain pounded incessantly, I went back to check on the fire, and rivulets of water had made their way to the flames. I made every attempt to keep the water from extinguishing the fire and realized that on some level I was trying to keep that fire alive, because of what it represented to me. When I gave up trying control the way it needed to go, the water slowly began to consume the fire, and I let it.

When it was about half gone, Duane came in, sat down in his usual place in the west, and simply said, "You saw him didn't you?"

He knew it.

We talked about that for some time, how the body leaves but the spirit often remains "making the rounds" and with the rain finally giving up, I put a pile of white birch bark on the glowing embers, and finally some hardwood that would last until the morning.

That night, and for the next three, I had "visitations" from JD in dreams.

I am on the side of a road, John on the other side, we began walking towards the middle, and there in the center, is a guitar case. He just looks at me, points to the case, then I wake up.

Second night all exactly the same as the first, but this time John opens the guitar case and hands me the guitar which is light as a feather. I wake up.

Third night all the same as the first two, but then he says to me, "My guitars are not where they are supposed to be." Then I wake up.

Finally, on the fourth night, all the same as the first three "visits" but now John beckons me to come "to his side of the road" and I am very reluctant. He understands and says, "Don't worry it's not your time." With that, I start to walk the expanse of road that is like wet asphalt and find myself sitting in a small cart next to the curb. John tells me I need to finish writing a song he started called, "Angels & Eagles" and when I am trying to figure out what he means, he produces a piece of paper, writes out the song in cursive with his left hand and gives it to me. He smiles and says, "Hang on." Then he proceeds to pull me in the cart to a stone entry way where he tells me to look inside.

I do, and up on the wall in glowing red letters is the word, **"TRUTH."**

I look at him, he says once again, "My guitars are not where they are supposed to be." I nod my head that I understand. He gives me a hug and says, "John, your voice matters."

Then, I wake up.

I sat with those dreams for a few weeks. In the meantime, I decided to present John's 1994 *The Wildlife Concert*, at a local theater as a tribute. As I recall, the theater owners were fans, so they said they would just open the concession stand and whatever people bought in the way of popcorn and candy, would be payment enough. So, the date was set, I talked about it on the radio for a few days, and then on the day of the event, I went over to swap out the laundry from the washer to the dryer, in the large barn main area, in the trailer park we lived in at the time, as we didn't have those appliances yet.

There wasn't anyone in the place, and it was all dark except for a couple of bulbs that lit the laundry area. I started to put the wet clothes from the washer into the dryer, when I heard a voice clear as a bell...

"I'm right behind you."

The voice startled me, and I quickly said, "I'm sorry, I'll move out of your way" but when I turned around there was no one. I called out. Again, no one in the building.

I hurried up, finished with the clothes and made the fifty-yard walk back home. In about thirty minutes I returned, this time the barn had people in it playing pool, and I quickly grabbed my clothes and headed back. I changed, and drove to the theater, not knowing how many people would even show up.

When I parked the car, I couldn't believe it.

There was a line out the door and far down the street. Eventually every seat was filled, I shared some of my memories and moments about John, Windstar, and when the program was over, I finished with the *Human Family* poem I wrote and delivered on stage in Aspen, three years before.

It was a bittersweet evening for sure.

Later, friends gathered at our house, some driving all the way from Chicago to be part of the celebration of John's life. At one point, one of those friends pulled me to the side and said, "I really enjoyed all that you shared, but I found that man standing behind you in the back corner of the stage a bit distracting. What was he doing there?"

Man? What man? Who did they see? Did anyone else see it?

"I'm right behind you." The words I had heard so clearly earlier that afternoon in the barn, came to mind

Not long after that night, I called someone close to John, and shared the ongoing dream about his guitars. He listened and finally said, "How in the world would you know about that?" He confided that there was some difficulty in locating the guitars.

Wow.

But, the full circle moment for all this, going back to that summer night in 1974, came 33 years later, when I produced and hosted a tribute show about John for *Oprah Radio* in 2007, ten years after his death. Annie Denver was my first guest, she shared her stories and unique perspective, along with many others including John's brother Ron, the late, great Roger "The Immortal" Nichols and his wife Conrad Reeder, the late, legendary producer Milt Okun, along with country singers Michael Martin Murphey and John Berry, as well as Hal Thau and the late Terry Lipman. The show was nominated for Peabody Award, and when I sent the finished program to Annie, I received a wonderful note about how she was able to listen to all of the songs and stories in context, as she drove around in the Rocky Mountains, and it was an important part of her healing process in dealing with the grief of John's death.

In 2009, Annie and a few of her friends were my guests at a taping of *The Oprah Winfrey Show*, and I had given Oprah's executive assistant Libby, a heads up about Annie attending. After the show was over, Oprah asked everyone to remain in their seats, announced that Annie was in the audience, and with that, "*You fill up my senses, like a night in the forest…*" welled from up the speakers in the studio, and the entire audience joined JD and Oprah in singing, *Annie's Song.*

I watched this moment unfold on the television in my office, mouth hanging open, tears in my eyes and felt that on some level, an important puzzle piece had been moved into place.

One year later, in 2010, Annie graciously hosted a book signing for me, when *Every Moment Matters* was published, and standing there, in the Rocky Mountains talking about my path, the lessons learned, and John's ongoing support and friendship to an SRO crowd at Explore Booksellers Aspen, was a capstone of sorts on one of the more foundational cornerstones in my life.

So here I sit, once again in awe of how the universal tumblers have moved things around in my life. All of the nuances and angles, shifts and changes, left turns and right corners on the journey, that guided me from mopping floors at a doughnut shop, to finding myself in the Rockies, as a best-selling author.

Truly...*phenomenal.*

But, what about all that "stuff" that is even more beyond explanation? Those dreams? The voice in the barn?

Whomever my friend saw behind me on the stage? Perhaps most of all, that hitchhiker named John, who showed up to sit in The Lodge for a time, until the storm had passed, and he could continue his journey?

I've long felt that when someone we are connected to passes on, we have a choice to take on a bit of their work, and surely John's friendship, support and influence in my life have compelled me to do just that.

I have learned to accept "responsibility" (or as I heard Chief Oren Lyons describe it, "our ability to respond") to that which has been asked of me. While there are times that I try to let go a bit, be more concerned about the latest box scores, or spend more time arguing over the headlines instead of always digging for lifelines, I am pulled back to "the work" as it were, that which seems to be the way I pay my rent for the space I take up on Earth.

So, every time I fired up the microphone on the thousands of radio shows over the years, or these days, for another episode of the *Life 2.0 Podcast*, or sit down to blog, or write another book, I roll back to that night in Boston, when John was able to see something inside me that was hidden, and needed to be brought forth.

And for that, I am truly grateful.

****

His longtime friend Tom Crum said it best, "I'm so very sad that John is gone, but so very glad he was here."

Me too.

JD

-8-

THE VISITORS

The first memory I have of a "visit" was in 1964, when I was six years old. At that time, my family lived in a massive two-flat building on the corner of Fletcher and Campbell streets in Chicago, a stone's throw from the legendary Riverview Amusement Park, and across the street from Material Service Corporation.

The building was laid out exactly the same on both the lower and upper floors, and I also remember that my mom and dad switched with my grandma Helen from downstairs to upstairs, which made zero sense to me, at least once as I recall. The inside back porch connected all the floors by a wooden staircase that went from the dreadful, damp, and mysterious basement (complete with coal storage bin) all the way up to the even more creepy attic, that was filled with all sorts of stuff, the dark corners a perfect place for monsters and other scary things to hide.

I never went up to the attic after dark. The basement? Absolutely no way. Even my dad had a hard time going down to throw coal in the stove, especially in the middle of the night.

I had just been tucked in the front bedroom off the living room on the 2nd floor. My mom closed the door, I was lying there thinking about things a little boy is concerned about (GI Joe, cartoons, baseball cards) when I heard what sounded like a tapping noise at the end of the bed. I sat up, and there was the outline of a person standing in front of the window, but inside the room. I clearly remember that the "body" was like that of the sort of static you would have seen on a television channel back in the day, a distorted black and white energy as if something was attempting to be "tuned in." I felt no fear at all but was mesmerized by this presence that seem to be checking in on me for some reason. Then, it slowly faded from sight and I went to sleep. There were two other times that this entity made an appearance, both times before my grandfather Carl passed away in 1965. It was just a fuzzy, reassuring image, with no discernable features, watching over me, as it felt back then. I have often wondered if it might have been my grandmother Laura, Carl's wife, who died when I was only two.

After he passed, I never saw it again.

****

Eight years later in 1973, my dad's father, Big John, passed away. He was a formidable fellow, a roughneck German and rouge of sorts, and my memories of him are fleeting at best, even though I was older when he died. At the wake, I was fascinated to see that my grandfather wore an earring. He had remarried later in life and after the funeral we all ended up at grandma Pearl's house, the adults having coffee and cake, the kids enduring it all by watching television. At one point in the evening, Pearl got up to check on us in the living room and she got to the entry way when she stopped in her tracks.

"OH MY GOD!" she yelled.

A great commotion took place, as we all rushed to the hallway, and there on the floor was a bunch of coins, nickels, dimes, and quarters, strewn about. Pearl insisted that all of the change had been on the dresser before she left earlier, and she was visibly shaken.

We all kinda just went back to our business, but less than an hour later, Pearl's mother heard a noise in the hallway, went to investigate and let out a scream that would wake the dead!

She said that she saw Big John standing at the dresser, as if he was looking for something, a spirit stuck in between dimensions perhaps. She quickly said, *"Peace be with you John."* and the figure instantly faded away.

These experiences became those "stories" that seemed to be right out of an episode of *The Twilight Zone* that were rolled out at poker parties, Thanksgiving, and other times when the adults got together, knocked back a few, and attempted to make sense out of the senseless.

****

While working on this chapter, I reached out to my Aunt Jo, and asked her if she had any "visits" during her time living at the big house on the corner. She said no apparitions had made their presence known, but to this day, more than a half century later, when she dreams of that house the focus is always on that same front bedroom where I had my encounter.

Huh.

A few years ago, my partner Teresa was doing some serious genealogy digging, and came across the fact that my great-grandfather Joseph (Big John's dad) died in that upstairs flat, back in 1954, four years before I was born. My dad and grandmother Helen were in California at the time, looking to possibly move there, when they got the call to come back to Chicago. Apparently, his death changed the course of their lives, instead of heading to the Golden State, they ended up back in the Windy City, where my dad eventually met my mom.

Huh #2.

Back to that bedroom. Was that my great-grandfather checking on me? My grandmother Laura? Some unknown previous tenant? All just an illusion?

As always, more questions than answers, for now.

****

There are times that the gateway for these visits are not limited to fuzzy figures in the hallway or a bedroom, but also on the phone.

I was a big wrestling fan as a kid, my dad had all the magazines, and after church on Sunday, my best pal Art and I could be found at the table in his kitchen, scarfing down apple slices and watching *Bob Luce Wrestling* from Chicago, on a little black and white television. Every week, all the greats were there. Nick Bockwinkle, Bobo Brazil, Pepper Gomez (The Man with the Cast Iron Stomach,) Wilbur Snyder, Dick the Bruiser and his "cousin" The Crusher, along with Yukon Moose Cholak, and Baron von Raschke, who would defeat opponents with one hand using, "The Brain Claw!"

So, when the opportunity came many years later, to do some work with the greatest tag-team in the history of pro wrestling (no offense to Bruiser and Crusher) The Road Warriors (Animal & Hawk) it was a like I had been prepared for the task on some level. I had a solid business background that worked well with some of the projects they had going, and for a few years the three of us did events, hung out, and took road trips until there were some changes in my life that had us moving in different directions. Before I go any further, on the record, the memories I have of those years are solid gold. Joe (Animal) was one of the most dedicated and innovative guys I have ever known and Mike (Hawk) was in many ways the exact opposite, a free spirit, perhaps dedicated a bit too much to things that weren't always in his best interest, but he had a heart as big as his biceps, and that I what I remember most.

On October 20, 2003, I got a voicemail message from Joe, informing me that Mike had passed away the day before. While I had not seen those guys in a few years, I was very sad to hear about his death, he was a larger than life character, always made my kids laugh, and while he had his demons, our conversations were always interesting, to say the least. Mike had been lugging boxes all day, decided to take a nap and died in his sleep of a heart attack at the age of 46.

I drove west across the UP of Michigan to Minneapolis to attend Mike's memorial service. It was quite an event, with wrestlers from all over the world filling the church, the foyer full of wrestling belts, awards, trophies, and pictures.

It was a moving tribute on every level.

I headed home the next day, more than a bit sad at Mike's passing, along with a bit of regret for the years inbetween that we hadn't stayed in touch. The drive back seemed twice as long, as the memories flooded forth. I thought about how much attention he gave my kids when he saw them (he was just a big kid himself) and the last road trip we took to Ft. Atkinson, Wisconsin for an event, years earlier, when Hawk, and the late Jim "The Anvil" Niedhart, and I ended up in a saloon, just before closing time, but that's another story.

By the time I got home, it was very late. Before I went to bed, I remember thinking, "I just need to know that Mike is okay." My brain was more than a bit fried, my body sagged after driving so many hours, and I was ready for a good night's sleep, so I was out like a light in no time.

Until the phone next to the bed rang at 2:58 a.m.

"*Hello*...hello?"

No one there.

Click.

I went back to sleep.

The next morning, I looked at the little caller ID on the phone (remember this was 2003, so it was advanced technology for the time) and it read, "Unknown."

Meh. No big deal. Wrong number.

The second night the phone rings at 2:59 a.m.

"Hello...hello...*hello*?"

Click.

I go back to sleep, same drill in the morning, check caller ID and it reads, "Unknown."

It happened again on the third night (3:00 a.m.), the fourth night (3:01 a.m.), and the fifth night (3:02 a.m.) By now I am getting pissed off, thinking some local yokel has my phone number and is calling from a nearby bar, just to get his jollies waking me up.

On the sixth day I finally called the phone company and since we had just bought the phones a few weeks before, the customer service rep suggested it might be some sort of glitch in the phone wiring or something. I asked if she would check the phone records to see if she could tell where the calls might be coming from.

After a few minutes she came back on the line and said *"Sir, there is no record of any incoming calls on your number on those dates and at those times."*

Excuse me?

She double checked. Nothing.

I hung up, my mouth hanging open, full well knowing that there wasn't anything wrong with the phones. It was like a scene in horror movie when someone finds out the calls are coming from *inside* the house.

Then, it hit me.

"I just want to know you are okay Mike."

That night, I went to sleep with a different perspective of the phone calls than I had the previous nights.

So, when the telephone rang at 3:03 a.m. I picked it up and said, "Mike, thanks for letting me know you are okay."

Click.

That was the last time the phone rang in the middle of the night.

A great relief came over me at that time, and all these years later, sitting at my computer recalling those incredibly sacred long-distance calls, makes me smile. Sadly, Joe passed away at the age of 60, in September of 2020, joining Hawk in Wrestling Valhalla.

****

As it turns out, "phantom calls" are not uncommon, and there are many documented cases of this phenomena, ever since the phone was invented. In 1920, Thomas Edison told a magazine that he had been, "building an apparatus to see if it is possible for personalities which have left this earth to communicate with us." The great inventor believed that when we die, our "life-units" were strewn about into the universe, and perhaps with the right communication device, a connection could be made.

I think Edison was on to something.

But there have been other instances in my life, that these visits came through a dream state of sorts, as well.

****

The last time I saw my mom alive was in early August of 1996. My family was in serious transition, leaving Chicago and heading to the UP of Michigan. The day we said goodbye to my folks, I clearly remember my mom hugging me in a way she never had before, much tighter and with a bit of affirmation of sorts, that on some level this move was the right thing to do, even though on paper, it was just this side of ridiculous.

My mom, while whipcord strong physically, had not been in good health for a very long time. She was an alcoholic and it took a serious toll on her, and the rest of us as well. I didn't know when she hugged me on that warm August evening, it would be our last hug, *but* not the last time I would see her.

Six months later, in January 1997, the phone rang at the Hillcrest Motel. As I described in previous chapters, it had been a challenging half-year to say the least. What I didn't need was anymore knocks on my heart, but sometimes there is just no way around it.

My sister was calling from Chicago, mom had died just hours before.

While I was caught off guard, I wasn't totally surprised, because eventually I knew that the pain that was consuming her, would eventually take her down. My mom was only 59 years old when she passed.

I talked with my sister about the arrangements, told her we would come down the next day, and to tell dad I would call him shortly.

But as I was talking with her, I was suddenly overwhelmed with fatigue, a heaviness that pushed down on me like a load of stone. I hung up the phone and went back to the rooms we lived in because I needed to lay down, and soon fell fast asleep. That's when my mom decided to visit me, in a dream, just minutes after she passed.

It was a warm summer day; I was looking out from the big porch swing at my boyhood home, towards the front yard. Green and growing, flowers, trees and birds. Peaceful, serene and glorious. I started gently moving back and forth on the swing, and then suddenly from the right end of the sidewalk, my mom comes walking down the street, wearing her favorite summer dress, looking young, beautiful, whole, and healthy. She keeps walking until she gets to the middle of the sidewalk, directly in front of me, stops and turns to look at me. She smiles wide, winks and then suddenly, her face is just inches from mine.

"I'm okay...and it's okay," she whispers to me.

I woke up and nearly jumped off the bed. I looked around the room, all was quiet and then that heaviness came on me again. So, I laid back down, fell back asleep and the dream repeated itself.

"I'm okay...and it's okay."

It was as if she was making sure I understood that while her body had enough, her spirit or "life-units" were still very active. By the time we got back to Chicago for her wake and funeral, there was a deep measure of peace that counterbalanced the sadness I felt.

****

In 2004, when it was my father's time, he came to me in a dream while he was battling in the final hours of his life in the hospital, 350 miles away in Chicago. I knew he was coming to the end of his journey and while we had patched up the wounds between father and son, I knew if I headed down to see him, it would be the last time, and I hesitated, not wanting to face the inevitable.

On a Thursday evening in late May, I went to sleep very early and immediately had a serious rewind back in time, to the big house on Berteau, the place my dad had made his castle for most of his life. I descended from above, to the front walkway and then up the familiar stairs, into the hallway, that was adorned as it was in the salad days of the mid 1970's, an enormous floor to ceiling bookshelf, jammed with every manner of literary work. The windows were open in the little dining area where we had our meals and then finally, I floated into the kitchen, filled with avocado green Sears appliances and the funny looking clock on the wall with a toucan bird on it.

When I started back towards the front door, the entire house began to turn gold around me with every step. It was like a flood of gold paint, drenching every single book, chair, picture and trophy. When I stepped on the porch, there was my dad, standing at the top step, wearing a hospital gown, arms bruised from needles, looking small, sad, and sick.

He held out his hands, as if he were a little boy.

"Butch, I want to go home."

I picked him up, he was light as a feather, he kissed my cheek and I woke up. I stuffed a few things in a suitcase and left at daybreak. Just two days later, he was gone.

John & Carol

****

Earlier in this book, you read about The Walk that was such a transformational piece of my journey. What follows, is in some ways a residual effect from that experience.

On the last week of my roundtrip journey to Chicago and back in 1996, I noticed a lump growing underneath my left eye at the top of my cheek. It was under the skin, and after two months on the road, it suddenly popped up. Thinking it was a serious zit, I set about attempting to put alcohol on it and then warm compresses but to no avail. So, I just ignored it, hoping it would just go away, because that works... *never*.

I finished The Walk the day before Thanksgiving in 1996, ate a huge meal the next day and slept for most of the next couple of days, letting familiar energy restore me on many levels. I'd been away from my family for a long time, we needed to reconnect, I'd lost a lot of weight during the journey, and hadn't slept well in a very long time, so it was a priority.

But that lump under my eye kept getting bigger and harder, and at the time, a trip to the doctor's office would be an expense that I didn't plan for, so I kept ignoring it. At some point, Bruce gave me a book called, *The Power of Your Subconscious Mind* by Joseph Murphy, published in 1963.

I read it and found a great many lessons in it, regarding the part of us that is buried deep, that rudder of beliefs that steers our ship, for better or for worse, no matter what things look like at the surface.

One chapter in particular focused on healings and that the subconscious mind would accept repetitive affirmations, which is how it builds the belief structures we call our reality. The example was given that the "life source" inside my body knew on some level how to help heal me, for its that very energy that is part of all life, which is ever changing, renewing, and growing. A prayer or mantra was suggested, that should be performed three times each day, once upon waking, in the middle of the day, and then just before sleep. A message to my subconscious mind that instructions being presented were to be followed.

I took Murphy's prescription, devised my own personal download and three times each day I proceeded to get still and open the deep file drawer of my beliefs, and insert instructions, "*My body was created by the Infinite Intelligence that is alive in my subconscious mind, and it knows how to heal me. This healing presence is now transforming every atom of my being, making me whole once again. Every piece of muscle, skin, tissue, organ and bone is in perfect working order. I give thanks for the healing of this body, and understand that the Spirit that dwells within, does the work."*

I did this every day, for nearly a month.

Then one night, I had dream in which a very tall man was standing up on a berm or rise in a dense forest. I could see him, a Paul Bunyan-like image with an imposing stance. I was standing in the forest clearing, he raised his right arm and when his hand was in alignment with my face, a bolt of electricity or lightning, came from his right forefinger as he said, "NO MORE!"

That beam of light hit me in the face, beneath my left eye and stayed there for what seemed like an eternity, and then I woke up.

It was morning, but everyone else was still asleep, so I crept into the small bathroom and looked in the mirror.

The lump was gone almost as if it had never existed.

There was no mark, scar or indent, just a slight dark patch where it had been.

To this day, I have no idea who or what that was in the dream, how it might have been conjured up, or why it chose a forest as its setting. What I do know, is that in the

24 years since I had that "connection" there was a healing, that has both baffled and amazed me at the same time.

And, finally, this brief, but very powerful encounter.

Back in 2001, I had been on the radio going on four years, and built up quite a listenership, had gotten a contract along the way that afforded me a salary, office, and a paid producer. For one year, I didn't have to worry about money, just concentrated on creating my show. When that contract ended, the station informed me they "couldn't sell me" and if I wanted to stay on the air, I had to figure out a way to pay for all of it myself.

Great.

I had no idea how to do that and yet, I knew that I was following what I was called to do, what I was "supposed" to be doing and yet, here was a major roadblock to that spiritual agreement.

My show was on live 3-6 p.m. Monday-Friday and I usually did all my show prep in the morning (or the night before) and then would head to the gym on the way to the station, get in a good workout, and a serious hot tub outing. I did more praying in that hot tub than I ever did in a church pew, something about being immersed in the water not only took the pain out of my joints, but also my spirit.

So, off I went to hit the weights, my mind full of chaos as to some way, shape or form to pull off what seemed impossible, find a way to stay on the radio. I had a good workout, got to the "prayer pool" to find it empty (always a good thing), and slipped into the hot water up to my neck. I boiled that way for a while, moved over to the sidewall where there was a ledge I could lean on, put my head on the tile behind me...and promptly fell asleep. (For the record, napping is not recommended in and around water of any significant depth.)

I had a dream of storm clouds thrashing about, lightning and thunder, pouring rain and howling winds. It was a twister, tornado, and cyclone all in one, the darkness only illuminated by the bolts of electricity that seemed to cut jagged slices out of the clouds at regular intervals.

It was without question a reflection of my state of mind in that moment.

Then, behind all of the storms, there was a looming presence, an expanding beam of light coming from a great distance. The clouds began to move apart a bit, like tectonic plates changing their alignment, until finally a familiar face was looking directly at me.

Walter Payton.

The NFL legend and greatest running back in the history of pro football, had passed away two years earlier, in 1999. Like many, his death stunned me, as if Superman had finally succumbed to Kryptonite.

But Sweetness wasn't very sweet during this visit.

His face was stern, eyes blazing, and jaw set hard. There was an overwhelming sense that he had come a long way to connect with me, he wasn't happy about it and when he spoke, his voice was iron-like in both cadence and tone.

"Don't you dare give up. You've come too far. If you quit now, you will never find your way in the world."

I woke up in that hot tub, forgetting where I was. No idea how long I had been in there, but incredibly no one else had walked in. It was as if I had been left alone, so that Walter could deliver his message.

I sat for a few more minutes, floating in the hot water, letting his words sink in. When I got to my office, I pulled out a picture of Walter and I from one of his golf outings. This was a smiling Sweetness, wearing a stunning blue jacket and broad grin, quite the contrast to what I had seen in my dream just an hour before.

His words were etched in my mind and I took them to heart. Eventually an idea came forth that would keep the show going and I was able to stay on the air for another year, until I donated a kidney to my daughter in 2002. The surgery coincided with a contract for my show to go national, but I had to turn it down in lieu of the impending procedure, a delay I gladly accepted, even though the timing was a bit interesting to me. Fortunately, I got picked up late in 2002 by the same company for a few months, but by then I needed a serious break and put the show on hiatus on New Year's Eve. I stayed off the air until the Spring of 2004, working on my first book, doing speaking events and spending time with my dad who passed away in May of that year.

Eventually, I would go back to my talk show, then over the years on to Oprah Radio, WGN and few other stops until the winds of change blew me in a new direction again, and these days I man the microphone via the Life 2.0

Podcast, a technology that didn't even exist when I started on the air in 1997.

While the "bully pulpit" of radio has changed for me over the years, I often feel that the best way I can say *"thank you"* to those who have inspired me along the way, is to maintain my vigil of attempting to make sense out of the senseless and digging to find the obvious truths buried in the utter absurdity of the times we live in.

The process of extracting lifelines from the headlines and clearing the way to common ground, and to not major in minor things along the way, all the diversions and dis-tractions, is never easy.

There have been many times that I have questioned my choice of career, especially when the voices of hate, an-ger and fear dominate the airwaves, but I have always honored the calling, come what may.

So, when I feel weary from the journey, attempting to figure out the business end of this podcast thing or if forging ahead is still viable at the age of 61, the ongoing ef-fort of writing one more book or taking on yet another pro-ject that in some way might move the human condition forward for the better, I often hear Walter's voice in my mind, with a message that still resonates with me all these years later…

"Don't you dare give up. You've come too far. If you quit now, you will never find your way in the world."

Sweetness

-9-

THE LITTLE GRANDMA

The common denominator that runs through every single one of the moments, memories, messages and other shit I can't explain is that I am never comfortable being a "spiritual conduit" or vessel that the events, experiences, or encounters demand of me without my conscious permission.

Most of these experiences have taken place when my mind is empty, after I have expunged myself of all distractions and simply occupy space as it were. That's when I'll get a download, a message or directions, that has zero to do with me, but is often "priority mail" for someone else. Then it's my choice to "deliver the mail" or not, a choice I take very seriously.

There was an incredible encounter six months after The Walk in the Spring of 1997. I was often asked to speak at area schools about my experiences and was always glad to oblige. One day after a presentation, I decided to walk over to my longtime friends Tom and Jessie's house. It was a beautiful, sunny early April afternoon, and I made the short walk to their house feeling light as can be. I had totally cleared out my mental hard drive and was hypersensitive to the sights, sounds, and feel of the moment. These times when I am so "*in the now*" and my thoughts are devoid of anything except what is in front of me, that I get a deep sense of calm and connectedness that seems to have me more transparent than the usual "thickness" I feel, bogged down by life with all the usual distractions.

I bounded up the front stairs, opened the outer porch door, went up to the main front door, knocked a couple times and then walked in. One thing about living in the UP of Michigan, locked doors were a rarity, (far different than living in Chicago) and those of us who knew each other simply showed up and made our presence known. Duane in particular, was famous for appearing right on time, especially when coffee was on.

As it turned out, I wasn't the only "visitor" that day.

I stepped into the front hall, and called out to Jessie who answered, "C'mon in John" from the kitchen. I took one more step and turned my head to the left and glanced through the glass of the closed French doors between the hallway and living room.

There, standing in front of a bookcase, was a short woman, dark hair swept back a bit, who seemed to be looking at all the things on the shelves. She had one hand on her hip, the other was pointing a book or something. She seemed to be on her tiptoes, wearing a white/grey dress of sorts, with pleasant features.

I figured Jessie had a guest over, no big deal.

When I got into the kitchen, I apologized for barging in and didn't want to interrupt the time she was spending with the lady in the living room.

"John, I am home alone. There is no one in the living room."

I thought to myself, that's not possible, I just saw her clear as day.

We went into the living room, and of course, it was empty. There on the shelf was a picture of a pretty dark-haired young lady, who looked very much like the woman that I saw standing in the room moments earlier. I had to ask the obvious question.

"Jess, who is that?"

"That's my Grandma Mary."

The words were hardly out of her mouth, before the download started to kick in. When I stood on the spot where I saw the lady, a torrent of words and thoughts came to me, jumbled, scratchy, but certain things were very clear.

The first message was that Jessie's mom, Barb, needed to be there (I found out while writing this chapter, that Mary had died from tuberculosis when she was just 29 years old and Barb was only six). Jess called her mom and dad who were first to arrive, then word spread and almost as if by some remote command, one by one Jessie's family began to show up. Her sister AnnMarie with her husband Jay was next, her brothers, then her sister Jeanne, all appearing at the house because they also felt that on some level, they needed to be there for some reason.

I asked Jess for a paper and pencil and began to write down what I heard and quickly realized that what I was writing was meant for each of them to hear.

So, there I sat in the living room, furiously writing as fast as I could, information that meant absolutely nothing to me, but apparently, at that time, a great deal to them.

I clearly recall that there was a great intensity to make sure that Jessie's mom spent time near the water. There was something about her connection to water that wasn't being fulfilled and I recall saying to her over and over again, "It's all about the water." The scribbling continued, little downloads for the family seated in front of me.

At one point I could clearly hear the word, "WATCH" and my first thought was to sit back and watch what was going to happen. Then came, "THE WATCH" which sounded to me like a book title or something and then finally, after a couple deep breaths, I wrote down, "THE WATCH IN THE DRAWER" and shared the message.

Jessie let out an audible gasp.

She had her grandfather's (Mary's husband) wristwatch in a dresser drawer in her upstairs bedroom.

The "intercession" seemed to go on for hours, in real time it was probably less than a half-hour. Then, as suddenly as it descended, it grew very quiet in my mind and with that, the energy simply lifted, the door was closed and I felt myself coming back into the room a bit, no longer "hollow bones" for what needed to take place.

****

While writing this chapter, I needed additional validation regarding this long-ago event, so I reached out to AnnMarie. She recounted that, "Many of us gathered there, including my ex-husband Jay. He sat across the room from me. We were nearing the end of a bad divorce. I remember while you were talking about things my gram had done, you turned to Jay asked about why he had so much anger and hostility inside. Your words caused him to open up and he cried about his childhood, it might have been the first time I ever saw that. I remember you telling me that I would do great things with my writing, and that my gram was proud of me. You also talked with Jeanne, too. That picture of my gramma looks very much like my brother Jimmy, and as fate would have it, me too."

****

I was exhausted, uncomfortable and a bit stunned at the paranormal gymnastics that had just been on display. An encounter of that magnitude takes a toll on me, and it's only happened a few other times to that extent. I always find myself sort of in-between two places when it happens, not sure of my footing in either one. I try to get out of the way, but there are times that my ego wants to know what's going on, and like a cell phone call that suddenly drops, done is done. I am also keenly aware that none of what comes through has ever been for me personally, even though I am very humbled by it all.

When I spoke with Jessie about this encounter, we each recalled pieces of the puzzle the other had forgotten. We agreed that it was nothing less than a divine intervention, a lifting of the veil, an opened channel, and a reconnection that had great purpose and was a major test of our belief systems, and my willingness to be the scribe, *like it or not.*

As I state many times in this book, *I don't like it,* mostly because it catches me so off-guard and once it happens, I want to keep it clean, not interfere and corrupt the file that is being downloaded. The part I do like, is that over the years, these sacred moments, messages, and memories have always reminded me that there is much more going on that I can possibly imagine, and that there seems to be great purpose to the time we are given, as long or brief as it may be.

This was the only experience I've ever had with what is termed "automatic writing" that was connected to some sort of phenomena. I literally felt a part of my mind open up, and fill with words in my mind's eye that I transposed to paper, as if I was some sort of spiritual Spirograph drawing kit, but with letters and words, not circles, symbols, and art. I was surprised (but that's on me) to find out that there are online courses that you can take (for a nominal fee of course) that can apparently teach anyone how to do this. In addition, you can also take a course in learning how to "talk with your spirit guides" for about $35 bucks.

Meh. No thanks.

For me, I only pay the price *when I don't listen*, but, when I do have the opportunity, and simply take the time be still within, the return on investment can be priceless.

Like on that warm, spring day, when the "little grandma" reached across time and space, to let her family know she was with them.

-10-

ETCHED IN STONE

At 6:30 in the morning on July 24, 1915, in spite of the steady rain, a massive crowd had gathered and was beginning to board the S.S. *Eastland*, docked at the Clark Street bridge on the Chicago River between Clark and LaSalle Streets.

It was by all accounts, a most anticipated event for thousands of employees of the Western Electric Hawthorne Works plant, based in Cicero, Illinois. They would be embarking on a boat trip across Lake Michigan to the 5th annual company picnic in Michigan City, Indiana. This was a very big deal to most of the employees, many of whom could never imagine taking a holiday such as this one.

The *Eastland* was known as, "The Speed Queen of The Great Lakes" and was one of five excursion boats along with *Theodore Roosevelt, Petoskey, Racine,* and *Rochester* that were chartered to take employees to the picnic for a day of relaxation and festivities. In some cases, entire families made their way onboard the *Eastland*, in anticipation of the celebration.

However, the *Eastland* had serious design flaws when it was built in 1902, one problem being it was very top heavy. There were two incidences shortly after the ship launched that involved a serious list, or lean to one side, and the ship was also damaged when it backed into a tug-boat in 1903. In addition, after the sinking of the *Titanic* in 1912, new rules placed lifeboats and preservers on the top deck, making the already unstable ship, even more treach-erous.

Shortly after 7 a.m. the ship was filled to capacity with 2,752 people onboard, many of them on the upper deck of the boat, standing on the port side (away from the dockside) to get a view of the river. Due to the weight im-balance, the ship began list towards the water, to which the crew opened the ballast tanks, so they could fill with water and put the ship back on a centerline.

It didn't work.

At 7:28 a.m., the ship suddenly lurched sharply away from the dock and rolled fully on its port side and began to sink rapidly in the murky water. Those who were on the top decks were tossed into the river, those who had moved below, were trapped inside, as the side of the ship came to rest on the bottom, only 20 feet below the surface. Those below decks were crushed by the sheer weight of the water, along with heavy furniture, pianos, bookcases, and trunks.

In spite of the quick response by the *Kenosha*, which was close by in the river, a total of 844 passengers and four crew members died in the tragedy.

In just fifteen minutes, 22 families were wiped out. The river filled with bodies of infants and children, teenagers and the elderly, and every age in between. Well-wishers and neighbors who had come to see their friends off on a holiday, ended up using gaff hooks and ladders to pull their loved ones out of the river. Eventually, divers were used to recover dozens of corpses, bystanders helped, laying the bodies out so they could be transported to the various morgues in the area, and by that afternoon, the remaining unidentified bodies were taken to the Second Regiment Armory on Washington Blvd, just a few blocks from the river.

The *Eastland* tragedy claimed nearly more than three times the lives than the Great Chicago Fire in 1871.

So, why the history lesson you might ask?

As it turns out, the Second Regiment Armory on Washington Street, where that makeshift morgue was set up, with blocks of ice next to the bodies of the *Eastland* victims, would eventually become Harpo Studios, home of *The Oprah Winfrey Show*.

I began working across the street from the main studio in 2006, developing and creating "Oprah and Friends" for SiriusXM radio, along with a stellar group of broadcasting professionals. I had great satisfaction in building the concept from the ground up to a viable satellite channel for about four years. As the senior producer of two daily programs, *The Dr. Oz Show* and *The Jean Chatzky Show*, along with Bob Greene's weekly hour on health and fitness, my team kept a serious pace, but we had a pretty good time doing it.

In October 2008, we were taping with Jean Chatzky, who was the Financial Editor of *The Today Show* at the time, in Edit 1, a small studio that we used mostly for postproduction, but was occasionally pressed into service to record shows as well. While normally her Oprah Radio shows had to do with money, for fun and something different I scheduled a Halloween show and being the pro, she is, went along with the program. So, Jean was locked in on an ISDN line (closed circuit dedicated line) from her home outside of New York, and on the guest phone line was my old friend the late, great Richard Crowe, aka "The Ghost Hunter," and life-long Chicago historian. I had met this remarkable man at the Alexander Robinson burial grounds that you read about in Chapter 3, many years before, and we had become good friends. So, when it was time to tape a Halloween episode for Jean's show, Richard was my go-to-guy.

For this particular outing we had Richard on talking with Jean about all the "haunted places" in Chicago, the stops he made as the guide of the "Supernatural Tours" which included the site of the St. Valentine's Day Massacre, the aforementioned burial ground of Alexander Robinson, searching for the ghost of Clarence Darrow by the Jackson Park lagoon, and perhaps the most famous of them all, Resurrection Mary, who is a hitchhiking ghost that picks up rides in the cars of unsuspecting gentleman, only to vanish, when they get to the gates of Resurrection Cemetery.

Scary shit.

The main reason I wanted Richard on the show was to talk about the *Eastland* tragedy and the numerous sightings of "The Grey Lady" in the lower level of the main Harpo Studios building, who is presumed to be one of the drowning victims, whose body was brought to the makeshift morgue back in 1915. Now and then, I would hear the security guys talking about some of the odd noises and things that were purported to be heard when they were walking the building - the sound of music and crying, and one of them mentioned that there was actually security camera footage of the apparition, caught on film as proof, however none of that stuff ever happened in the building I worked in, located kitty-corner across the street from the main building.

Or, so I thought.

During this particular recording session, there were three and sometimes four of us crammed into the little edit suite, myself, Katie - my board op/editor, Teresa from legal, and Matt - one of our engineers who always kept a tech vigil whenever we were taping via ISDN.

Richard had done a great job of sharing some of his more "chilling moments" with Jean, who took it all in stride. So, we wrap up the show, thanked Richard for his time and dedication, let him go on the phone, and closed off that line. We're having small conversation, via a talkback speaker with Jean on the closed-circuit line, Katie is mixing down the audio clip, Matt and Teresa are hanging out as we get ready to tape the next show and that's when it happened.

A distended voice fills the room...

"NIELS PETERSEN WILL NOT BE FORGOTTEN!"

WHAT WAS THAT?

THEN IT HAPPENS AGAIN! It sounds like it's coming from a small auxiliary speaker that isn't turned on or being used in any way, shape or form.

"NIELS PETERSEN WILL NOT BE FORGOTTEN!"

We all just sat there with our mouth's hanging open, even Jean heard it through the talk back line, all the way in New York.

"WTF was that?" I said.

Katie's eyes were as big as saucers, Teresa didn't know quite what to say, Matt being the guy he is, scribbled down the name we all heard.

The crew needed a time out, and I opened the door to the little room, letting some fresh air in, and whatever the hell that was…*out.*

Word of the "encounter" spread fast, and after another check of the wiring, with regards to recording and editing, it was determined that there was no way for a voice from any other outside (or inside) source to have come through that speaker, that wasn't even turned on.

Eventually, we resumed taping Jean's show with the door open, and that was the end of it.

For about three hours.

Later that afternoon, Matt comes into my office and says, *"You're not gonna believe this…"* He had dug through the list of victims that died in the *Eastland* disaster.

"Petersen, Niels (Nelson) Rasmus, 46 years old, married, Danish, buried in Oak Ridge Cemetery. Foreman, Western Electric Company."

Unbelievable…and yet…*we all heard it.* From a speaker that wasn't even plugged in to the audio board.

I don't know how long it took for us to start using that edit suite again, or how many times I turned on all the lights if I was working late at the studio, but to this day, if I bring up that "visit" with those of us that were there, the hair on my neck stands up.

So, what was that all about?

All these years later, I'm still not quite sure.

Shortly thereafter, I started digging into Electronic Voice Phenomena (EVP) which are sounds found on electronic recordings that are interpreted as *"spirit voices"* that have been either unintentionally recorded or intentionally requested and recorded. It was the famed Parapsychologist Konstantīns Raudive, who popularized the idea in the 1970s, and described EVP as typically brief, usually the length of a word or short phrase.

But if that is the description, we weren't requesting the presence of Niels Petersen, or anyone else for that matter. The short phrase thing fits, and as I recall the voice was clear, concise, matter of fact, as if making a declaration of sorts, and that multiple people heard it is unusual...as if what, hearing voices from a speaker that isn't plugged in is...normal?

Whose voice was it? What about Mr. Petersen shouldn't be forgotten?

Later that week, I finally mustered up the courage to call Richard at his office and share what happened. He wasn't at all surprised, thought it was a very cool experience and told me to let him know if it happened again.

I assured him that he'd be the first person I called, but once was more than enough for me.

As I began to make a list of experiences I've had, that would eventually become chapters in this book, including those that multiple people witnessed were of a high priority to me. It's one thing for me to have a dream, visit, or other unexplained phenomena, but quite another for a "group encounter" like this one, that in my opinion, lends credibility and credence to the overall message and intent of this book

And what is the message exactly?

There is far more going on than meets the eye, and for whatever reason, at times the "veil" between "here" and "there" is often very thin. These experiences, while at times unnerving, are somehow "normal" when it comes to the lingering life force of energy that each of us carries while we are alive, and apparently can still manifest after we are long gone.

The former Harpo Studios was leveled, and is now the headquarters of that fast-food chain with the golden arches that sells billions of burgers. Not sure what is across the street where our radio studios used to be, as I don't get over to that part of the city much. I often wonder if all that digging in the ground, at the site that at one time held the bodies of so many that died tragically in the *Eastland* disaster, has further disturbed those who seemed to be spiritually interred there, even though their bodies are buried elsewhere.

I wouldn't be one-bit surprised if they make their presence known in some way, shape or form.

While writing this chapter, it was on me big time to locate the Oak Ridge Cemetery and as fate would have it, it's very close to where I live, a short 10-minute walk. We did a little digging (absolutely no pun intended) and found Niels in Section 12, plot 96. As it turns out, he is buried there with his little four-year-old son, Royal, who drowned along with father. His wife, Viola, survived the horror of the *Eastland*, buried her husband and boy and after a second marriage and restarting her family, died at the very young age of 37.

At first, seeing their names on that grave marker sparked a deep sense of sadness, as I wondered if anyone had visited their resting place in the past century, and then came a feeling of "mission accomplished" as the only reason I was even standing on that spot, was because of a distended voice on a radio speaker over a decade ago.

Over time, their stone had been slowly sliding off its base, so I moved it back to its original position, scraped off the lichen and dirt, cleaned out the deep grooves worn into the marker and oddly enough, if you view the memorial from the side it's a book carved in stone, with Niels and Royal's names etched on the pages.

To that end, I now make routine visits to the resting place of this father and his son. It gives me a chance to take a few minutes to think about that July day, 105 years ago, when there was no way Niels and little Royal could have known that it would be their last, and that they would be buried side by side for eternity.

And, if nothing else, because you are reading these words and seeing their names, if only for the length of this chapter, they are in fact, not forgotten.

-11-

MOTHER MARY

One of the more interesting, but frustrating things as an author, is that I often have to wait for a chapter to "write itself" as opposed to me sitting down in some sort of Stephen King like fashion and knocking out ten pages a day, come what may. Every single chapter in this little book, had a point of impact in my life many years ago, and then the ripple effect takes place, sending concentric rings into my consciousness with a lesson, or forgotten message years or even decades later.

Such was my "encounter" on a well-traveled divided highway in Wisconsin, with the Blessed Virgin Mary.

Yea...I know. But first, this disclaimer.

While I was baptized in the Catholic Church, I have no recollection of any formal (or informal) religious studies with the exception of learning to recite the "Lord's Prayer" as a boy, and a short stint at St. Edward school in Chicago, mostly because I liked the ties they wore. No deep background in my family as regular church-going folk, no first five row Catholics, no get on your knees before bed and say your prayers sort of upbringing. Matter of fact, one of my biggest religious influences came from a minister, not a priest. The late, great Rev. Bob G. Sills was a thundering presence at the Irving Park Presbyterian Church, where my Cub Scout meetings were held and I eventually was recruited to play on the basketball team. B.G. would often recount his "wake up call" while picking cotton in the south, as "God tapped him on the shoulder" and called him into the ministry. Bob was a modern-day Teddy Roosevelt of sorts, a broad, gapped toothed smile under a flowing white moustache, barrel chested, and would often show up in the pulpit with a blue leisure suit and white boots under his robes.

He was quite a sight, and his conviction for living up to what he was called to do, has stayed with me since I was probably 12 years old.

That's all the religion I had growing up. I wasn't surrounded by images or icons of the Catholic persuasion, and as I think on it now, the most "religious" person was my great Aunt Eleanor, who recited scripture and psalms very early in the morning when she lived with us in her later years. I can still recall hearing her whispering those prayers, before dawn, through the shared heating vent that kept both our bedrooms warm. She was a devout Lutheran; and I still have that Bible she read from every morning and evening.

But it's more of a keepsake for me, than my "daily bread" as it was for her.

So, that's why when this "intervention" took place, it was not only jarring, unnerving, and extremely emotional, it was also unsettling in the fact that I don't have the formal blueprint on paper to have this sort of connection to an image, that while very powerful for some, had near zero meaning to me- there is no file drawer in my mind, that I am aware of, marked "The Virgin Mother" filled with pictures or prayers to the mother of Jesus Christ.

In October 2008, I was driving from Chicago north back to my home in the Upper Peninsula of Michigan, after another week of work as the Senior Producer of *The Dr. Oz Show* on *Oprah Radio*. I made the weekly roundtrip drive north and south, about 800 miles back and forth, racking up the miles big time. It was a therapy of sorts, from the grinding production of radio, the pressure that comes with working under the brand name of the most recognized woman in the world, along with the push and pull of the usual day to day stuff that fills my brain bucket. I could put my '99 Olds Aurora on cruise control and let the city energy slowly drain off of me as the miles rubbed off the stress.

It was warm for fall; the leaves were changing which made the drive all that more enjoyable. I headed into the town of Marinette, Wisconsin, on US 41, where the four-lane highway becomes a two-lane road into town. I had the sunroof open on the car, was feeling very relaxed, after completing three hours of my five-hour drive.

I slowed down to about 40 miles an hour, when I was about to pass a local cheese market I happened to glance across the highway towards the place, which was about 50 yards away, when it happened.

There standing just south of the entrance to the market was...*THE BLESSED VIRGIN MARY*.

It was a fleeting image. She stood there with arms raised up, resplendent in white and with a faint glow of yellow around her, like a doorway of sorts. I was instantly overcome with emotion. Tears came forth and I had to catch my breath.

My line of sight was blurred, but I heard these exact words in my head very clearly... *"THE BLESSINGS OF THE WALK WILL COME NOW..."*

And then, the apparition was gone just as quickly as it appeared.

I was a wreck, (and didn't want to cause one,) so I pulled over to the side of the road, overcome with emotions that I now struggle to describe accurately in words. I decided to call Duane. Twelve years earlier on The Walk, we had crossed very spot where the Blessed Virgin Mary appeared to me, and if anyone could understand what just took place, it would be him.

I'm glad he answered the phone, because I cannot imagine what sort of message I would have left, it probably would have gone like this:

"Hey Duane, it's John. Listen, I was just driving back north on US 41 and The Virgin Mother appeared to me and said, 'the blessings of The Walk will come now' and I am in major overwhelm, unable to think clearly or drive because I can't stop crying. So, if you get this message in the next five minutes, give me a call." ·

When Duane answered the phone, I basically blubbered through tears about what I had seen, the enormous warm energy that enveloped me, and the spiritual shock to my belief system that had me repeating the words that I "heard" from this vision appearing to me, outside of a cheese shop, hardly the place I would imagine a divine intervention.

After I shared what happened, he took a very long pause on the other end of the phone and simply said, "Yep."

"YEP?"

However, to understand his response, you have to know a bit about Duane's background.

In a very different time, Duane knew his way around the bars, and one night he came home to find a bag of trash that hadn't been taken out and kicked it all over the porch. This brought out his young son Aaron (also known known as *Mukwa Ogema*, or *Bear Chief*) who admonished his father for his actions and suggested that he "*go to the fire*" on his cousin Bruce and Pat's property in Rapid River. Standing in front of the fire, not knowing what to do, he began to pray to find a way to his "*true self*" and thus began a journey that would take him deep within his soul and eventually to the far corners of the world.

Duane was given the name *Mukwa Oday*, (which means *Bear Heart)* and he became a "Drum Keeper," one who is the guardian of the sacred songs and the builder of drums for ceremony, celebration, and remembrances. The many drums Duane has crafted by hand, are spread far and wide all over the world, ensuring that the heartbeat of Mother Earth remains strong and in the spirit of people from all walks of life.

His travels with Bruce have brought him to major cities, small towns, and international locations like The Hague, Paris, Peru, and Russia providing the songs and sounds for countless sacred fires. To me, Bruce and Duane are the Ralph Kramden and Ed Norton of spirituality. A down to earth, plain speaking tag-team that travel the world leaving a trail of hope, faith, teachings and laughter wherever they go.

I've been fortunate to know some really incredible people, but these two men, who have changed so many lives for the better, because they first changed their own, are the very definition of the "ripple effect."

Duane

For 33 years, Duane worked at a paper mill in Escanaba, Michigan and every shift he would cross the Esky
River and make an offering of tobacco, sending his prayers
for the people and the planet directly into the life blood of
Mother Earth. Now retired, he continues his work on behalf of the people, making drums, protecting the spirit of
the songs he has been given and the voices of the ancestors
that come through him. He remains a testament to the
power of spiritual evolution, along with honoring and
sharing the traditions of his and Bruce's teacher, the late
Dale Thomas, *Nowaten* (He Who Listens).

So, just saying *"yep"* carries a lot of weight with it.

Whereas my Presbyterian mindset wanted an answer right now for this or any other experience, Duane always says, *"you have to let it take the time it takes."* He (and Bruce) would often sit with one word, *for a year*, just studying and learning from the many nuances and lessons that word might offer them.

Maybe that's part of the lesson.

When you least expect it, with the firewall of the ego down, unaware and without expectation, is when the "spirit" can best find its way to us.

These sightings are termed a "Marian apparition" which is reported as a supernatural appearance by the Blessed Mother.

I'm not gonna take up space attempting to decipher the spiritual or religious implications of what took place, but the difference between "believing" in what happened and "knowing" is simple to me. A *belief* is the acceptance of something conceptual without direct evidence to support it, a *knowing* is a concrete, constructive experience that is visceral. Seeing the Virgin Mother on a highway in the Badger State, was way past gazing at some icon in a church, or holding a rosary or prayer card for me.

It was visceral in the *extreme*.

While my "inner spirit" has accepted this event as true, my mind needed more in an attempt to rationalize that which is totally irrational.

So, I did a bit of research for some insight and information on the subject. According to Professor Sandra L. Zimdars-Swartz since the increase in Western Christianity in the 10th and 11th centuries the figure most often seen has been the Virgin Mary.

Robert Orsi, author of *The Madonna of 115th Street,* states that, "An apparition is a conjunction of transcendence and temporality where the transcendent breaks into time."

That definition certainly fits my experience and helped me put into words that which took place on that autumn afternoon.

To this day, I have no idea what "the blessings of The Walk" are or if they have shown up and if they did and I missed them, or if they are showing up in ways I do not recognize because my human ego is looking for blessings that are "worthy" in my limited judgment. The words I heard that day, are an open-ended declaration and invitation to me, the source of which is still clearly visible in my mind's eye. I often have to remind myself, to keep my heart and mind open to blessings, both great and small.

There is an old saying about "blessings in disguise" those unforeseen, often tragic events or experiences, that in time prove to be something of great value and have a positive outcome.

"The blessings of The Walk will come now"

To that end, I suppose it's all in how I view my journey since that afternoon, just over a decade ago. As my late, great, friend Wayne Dyer would say, *"When you change the way you look at things, the things you look at change."*

Has there been some rough waters since that day on the highway? Absolutely. Have I faltered on this path more times than I can count, or is it all in perfect order? Is the blessing of seeing the sunrise this morning part and parcel of the reminder that in the end, just as in the beginning, blessings are all around us, but often go unnoticed until we are pushed to see them?

Perhaps.

-12-

CHELSEY'S WINDOW

My first book, *Living an Uncommon Life* concludes with the chapter entitled "Love Lights The Way" about the death of 16- year-old Chesley Jo Hewitt on February 26, 2002. A logging truck slammed into the car she was driving with her boyfriend, 17-year-old Timothy Wotchko, who was in the passenger seat. Chelsey died at the scene, and Tim passed one day later, on February 27th, but he lived long enough to become an organ donor, something he discussed with his mom, just a couple of weeks before he died. They were on their way to a local basketball game where Chesley was going to sing the National Anthem before tip-off.

I was on my way home after doing three hours of radio, snaking my way back on the Upper Michigan roads, laden with snow, which was typical for that time of year. I wasn't in the house more than five minutes, when the phone rang, and I got the news. I headed to Duane's house, where kids were gathering, looking for a place to share their shock and grief. When I arrived, it was just as you would imagine, overwhelming sadness at the news of Chelsey's death. When word came the next day that Tim had also died, the pain was beyond measure, it was as if a bomb of darkness had been dropped in the hamlets of Gladstone and Rapid River, creating of ripple unfathomable grief.

Not too long after the kids had passed, Tim's dad Denny began building a sauna in his backyard, a place where he could sweat out the pain that was bone marrow deep. All the building materials just kind of "showed up" and soon enough, a sturdy, wood, stone and metal structure stood in place. The stove was installed, and at night, when the sanctuary was lit, the glass block window in the wall in the shape of a cross, illuminated the night.

Most times there were four of us in the sauna, all fathers, and all there with one simple mission. To sit with Dennis and Chelsey's dad Doug, while they attempted to quench pain inside their hearts. Pour after pour of cold well water on the heated stones brought forth a steam that would permeate even the thickest sorrow, if only for a couple hours. For two years, every Wednesday evening, without fail, we sat in that sauna, in the dark, crying, laughing, singing, and sweating.

Then, it was Doug's turn.

He found a spot in his yard that would be perfect for a sauna. The idea for his place came from a book that touted the effectiveness of sawdust as an insulation factor in-between the logs and mortar the walls would be built of. My few years of concrete experience was put into play when the foundation was poured, then Doug and Duane, perhaps the two handiest guys I know, took care of the big stuff. When the structure was complete, it was a sight to behold. It didn't take long once the cast iron stove insert was fired up, to realize that this sauna was a very different sweat than we previously experienced.

Denny's sauna was like a super-heated shop-vac of sorts, squeezing and sucking every drop of water from my body. It was serious dry heat, even when making a pour on the rocks, the moisture was quickly absorbed by the wood and metal. Doug's sauna was more like an infusion of heat and water, an injection of sorts, even though profuse sweating was inevitable. I would come out of Denny's feeling cleansed but like a piece of rawhide left out in the sun;

finishing up at Doug's I always felt refreshed, like I just spent a couple of hours in the ocean.

Both saunas served an important purpose, the "*yin and yang*" of energy at work, deep removal and just as deep restoration. I consider both of these little retreats to be sacred because of why they were built, the brotherhood that gathered to help one another heal, the combination of elements that were put in place from the ground up, and that holy baptism that took place every time someone said, "I need to make a pour."

For ten years, without fail, the "Naked Men's Club" convened at one or the other of these two portals every Wednesday night. Over that time, Duane would add piped in music and interior lighting at Doug's and Denny had a journal filled with thoughts and a great area to just sit and cool down. It became nothing less than a sacred ritual, a place for us to cleanse our mind, body, and spirit of the rust that builds up just from being alive, and the ongoing process of two fathers looking to make sense out of the senseless.

While the conversations were incredible, the prayers formidable and the cleansing life affirming, there was one "incident" in the Naked Men's Club, that totally puts me in league with those who know that life does not end, it just changes form.

It was in the winter of 2013 and this particular Wednesday stands out as bone chilling cold, which you get used to living in the UP, but after a time, the only relief is to fire up the stove, get the water going for those pours, and watch the thermostat work its way up to our preferred temperature of about 185 degrees, which will melt sorrow away until it's time to face the world again.

We were at Doug's place; the fire had been lit a couple hours earlier because the sauna needed extra time to warm up due to the cold. We all brought some chow, Doug would put on a pot of coffee and we would feast on everything from dinner leftovers, to hard salami, to cookies, to BBQ chips - you know - *healthy stuff*. I would usually bring a gallon of water with me, trying to keep my levels good, but there was nothing better than coming out and downing an ice-cold Coke Zero, that I had buried in a snowbank before we went in.

The Naked Men's Club

That night the lineup was Doug, Duane, me, along with a fairly new recruit, Padre Paul, who is a Lutheran minister, but looks more like an offensive tackle for the Green Bay Packers. When Paul began attending the NMC, he brought a whole new perspective to our efforts, and took up a fair amount of room as well.

Once we got settled in, a few pours were made and as the steam rose, Doug began to talk about something that was really bothering him. As it turns out, a friend of the family, who went to school and graduated with Chelsey, had been having a recurring dream for a very long time.

In the dream, Doug would walk out on the stage of their high school auditorium, very sad, and tell everyone in the audience, "*I can't see Chelsey. Can you please help me find her?*" Then suddenly, from the other side of the stage, Chelsey would walk out and say, "*Here I am Dad,*" and they would hug each other until this girl woke up. Finally, 11 years after Chesley's death, the friend shared the dream with Doug, and while he found some comfort in it, it also made him really angry.

Doug shared with us how he felt "left out" of so many of the experiences that other people had around Chelsey. He wanted to know why, as her father, he wasn't having a dream like that, why he was the one that kept looking without any sort of "connection" being made, or was seemingly unable to find any reason whatsoever that the comfort that the friend got from the dream, was not available to him. The more he talked, the tighter the circles got with his words, grinding on each other, ramping up serious energy. It was good to let him vent, *without judgement*, a rare commodity.

Duane then offered his spiritual perspective on the matter, backed up by Padre Paul from the more formal religious aspect, and in just a few minutes, it was like a tag-team of energy, both filled with truth, both overflowing with ideas, thoughts, and even some scripture.

That's when things started to get really interesting.

I noticed a faint, red glow on the wall of the sauna behind where Doug, Duane, and the Padre were seated. I had stretched out on the far wall, grabbing a chance to simply lie down in the blistering heat. My first thought was that the glow was from the iron stove, which if heated to near 190 degrees, would be glowing red hot. But this was *behind the guys*, not in front of them. I did a double take and it appeared to me that the glow was actually coming off of Doug's back itself!

WTF?

The more he talked, the more his back glowed in the dark, a deep crimson red, like some sort of human firefly.

That's some weird shit right there.

I rolled back over, Duane and Paul were still hammering away with their good intentions and I stuck my nose as close as I could to the wall, finding a cool spot as several more pours had been made. If you have never been in a sauna like this, while invigorating, the pours and steam can not only open your pores, but also fry your brain, or at least that's what it feels like, and frankly that's what I thought was happening to me.

That's when I heard a voice, a female voice, *"Go look at the window."*

What was that? What? *What?*

I remained still, unsure of what I had heard.

There was no "out of body" experience, just a quiet whisper that I could discern underneath the voices of the guys talking, just a couple of feet away.

I waited a few minutes. They kept talking, making pours, the stones sizzled, the red glow remained.

What window? The window on the door leading into the sauna? Was it the little sliding window on the outer wall of the building that we used to vent the changing room? What about Chelsey's bedroom window?

I recalled her room was on the 2nd floor, towards the garage side of the house. So, I got up, rinsed off in the shower, exited the main sauna room to dry off and then take a look out of the front door at that upstairs window.

I never made it that far.

There, on the inside of the main entrance door window, that was covered in condensation, were the following words, as if someone had used a finger to etch them on the wet glass…

I LUV U DAD

I dropped to one knee. My mouth went dry, even though I had been guzzling water, I became incredibly emotional and actually lost my breath for a moment or two.

Slowly I steadied myself and went back into the main sauna. The guys were still yammering, and I told them they needed to stop because there was something that Doug needed to see.

We all walked back out; the words were still there as if they were permanently engraved in the glass.

It was Doug's turn to drop to his knees.

Instantly, his back was no longer red.

We all stood there in awe of this "visit" and it was Padre Paul who broke the silence with, "Do you think we should take a picture of this for proof?"

It wasn't about proving this to anyone else, it was clearly a message for Doug, from Chelsey.

As we stood and witnessed this phenomenal expression of love, I asked Doug if he was okay.

"I am now" he said quietly.

We were locked on that spot, for what seemed to be an eternity, not wanting to move, for fear of cracking the seal on what was a most phenomenal event, something so far past the boundary of what couldn't possibly be explained to anyone, without sounding like insane men. But all of us are fathers, and hardy souls, and we knew what we knew in that holy moment, as the evidence was literally right before our eyes and etched on our hearts as well.

Finally, Duane, Paul and I dried off and dressed, gently opened the door and excused ourselves, leaving our brother Doug to spend precious time with the energy of his daughter.

For the record, there was nobody home when we took the sauna, no one walked in, heard our conversation, and took it upon themselves to use a finger to "write" that message. Just the four of us, inside, but apparently not totally alone.

****

Chelsey Jo

When I asked Doug for his permission to include this experience in the book, he said, "Anytime someone can read about Chelsey, I am good with it." Then, while I was in the middle of this chapter, I called him to confirm, verify and recall some of that night. We ended up talking for a quite a while, about what is most important in our lives, what we spend time on, what distractions we should avoid and how in the end, just as in the beginning, there are some experiences to which there is no rational answer to.

They are just gifts, and if there is an explanation, an answer, perhaps it's that the love of a daughter for her father, can absolutely transcend time and space.

That cold winter night in the Naked Men's Club was truly an extraordinary experience and with the handwriting literally on the glass, it became very clear that we are never really alone.

It is a moment frozen in time for the four of us, and a lesson, teaching and reminder, that those who have gone before us, are still with us and only a thought away.

Postscript

I keep a copy of Ralph Waldo Emerson's book, *Self-Reliance and Other Essays* close at hand. Nestled in the chapter "Spiritual Laws" my favorite quote from this timeless teacher resides.

"The whole course of things goes to teach us faith. We need only obey. There is guidance for each of us, and by lowly listening we shall hear the right word. Place yourself in the middle of the stream of power and wisdom which flows into you as life, place yourself in the full center of that flood, then you are without effort impelled to truth, to right, and a perfect contentment."

The emphasis for me is on *"guidance for each of us, and by lowly listening we shall hear the right word."* Every experience I have shared in this book is somehow linked to the *"listening"* Emerson insisted is a critical component of living a life that is worth putting on paper.

Even as I wrap up this book, the evidence still comes to mind in short bursts to underscore that teaching. Like the time my friend Ginny invited me to lunch, and when I was getting my jacket out of the closet I clearly heard, *"take your spare car keys."* Of course, I brushed it off. There is no way to explain however, that just an hour later, my keys vanished at a small restaurant, and even though the staff dug through the garbage and I was literally on my hands and knees searching the booth cushions, they were no-where to be found. Ginny ended up having to drive me 60 miles round trip to Chicago and back, so I could get the ex-tra set of keys, for my car, that I had to leave sitting in the lot.

I *heard* the right words but didn't *listen* and certainly didn't follow instructions. Just one of the many times my inner GPS had me pointed in the right direction, but I ig-nored it in favor of my ego mind.

While that "guidance" has come to me in many forms, it's always been little bits and pieces of a much big-ger puzzle. Putting this book together and sharing some of these incredibly sacred events, has not only given me a chance to gain new perspective on "old" experiences, but also has solidified to me that on some level, I've been on an incredible journey, for which I very humble, grateful and fortunate.

To be clear, while the sacred moments, messages, memories and other shit I can't explain have enhanced my life experience, it hasn't made it any easier at times, because growth is usually a painful, uncomfortable process, as that which hurts, also instructs. These experiences then, are the kaleidoscope that gave me a richer, more colorful and intense view of life than I could have ever imagined, even in the midst of difficulty and loss.

In closing, I leave you with a reminder of how important it is to pay attention to the signs, listen for the whispers, never ignore the nudges, keep your eyes and ears open, and most importantly... your heart.

If you go within, you will never go without.

Safe travels.

JSA

ABOUT THE AUTHOR

John St. Augustine is a sought-after speaker on understanding and improving the human condition, he has presented at TEDxNASA and TEDxOntario, along with hundreds of platforms, corporations and public events both nationally and internationally.

He is a best-selling author, multi-award-winning broadcaster, producer, media consultant, ghost-writer, and currently the host of The Life 2.0 Podcast. For more information go to www.auroramediaproductions.com

CPSIA information can be obtained
at www.ICGtesting.com
Printed in the USA
LVHW091123110421
684152LV00021B/208